BASTARDOGRAPHY

BASTARDOGRAPHY

Simon Jay

ZITEBOOKS
LONDON

Published by ZiteBooks 2016
www.zitebooks.com

ISBN 978-1-910697-04-7

Copyright © ZiteBooks 2016
Copyright © Simon Jay 2016
Cover design © flamin ape 2016

The right of Simon Jay to be identified as the author of this work has been asserted by him in accordance with the Copyright, Designs and Patents Act 1988.

Cover photograph by Simon Jay
Inner Sleeve photographs by Chris Rogers (front) and Alice Dollé Nicol (back)

All rights reserved. No part of this publication may be reproduced, stored in or introduced into a retrieval system, or transmitted, in any form, or by any means (electronic, mechanical, photocopying, recording or otherwise) without the prior written permission of the publisher. Any person who does any unauthorised act in relation to this publication may be liable to criminal prosecution and civil claims for damages.

Some of the names and places in this book have been changed to protect people. All events described are the truthful recollections of the writer. In all instances of quotation, every opportunity has been made to contact the author.

A CIP catalogue record for this book is available from the British Library.

Typeset by flamin ape
Printed and bound in Great Britain by CPI Group (UK) Ltd, Croydon, CR0 4YY.

ZiteBooks has a band of writers from around the world to challenge the imagination of readers.
We publish in ebook and hard copy format on Amazon.

To find out more visit: www.zitebooks.com

ACKNOWLEDGEMENTS

Thank you to Mattie Alston and Michael Higgins for being so enthusiastic and reading significant parts of an early draft with encouragement and kindness. To the amazing Patty Dohle for her offer of proof-reading *gratis* and for being an excellent friend with a view to getting me out of potential litigation; much appreciated. Thank you to Scott Payne who was one of the many who encouraged me to continue when I told him privately that I didn't want to. To my parents and sister for being an amazing family and for not disowning me when they read it. To Matt Reynolds who is a bigger fan of my own work than I am, which takes some beating; I am sure he'll be using this tome for research into his media theory biography on my work *Jacktion*. To Alice Dollé Nicol for reminding me of the beauty of art in my efforts to create it, as well as providing the Mapplethorpesque dust jacket photo.

Eileen Roy needs special mention for keeping me buoyant and believing in me; effectively being my patron these last few years. Biggest thank you of all to Martin Godleman who was forever on at me to write a book about my life that I didn't want to write and then really wanted to write, and for being patient with me when it fell overdue. And finally one last thank you to Emma David, my partner in mental health pursuits. Your little Mildred done good.

For Ben.

CONTENTS

Definition

Preamble

Chapter One - Birth	*1*
Chapter Two - Pocahontas	*18*
Chapter Three - Madness Foreplay	*24*
Chapter Four - School Outing	*30*
Chapter Five - Drapers	*55*
Chapter Six - Age of Aquarius	*69*
Chapter Seven - Nancy	*81*
Chapter Eight - Yoof Groups	*87*
Chapter Nine - Parasites, Flats and College	*109*
Chapter Ten - Salad Cream Days	*133*
Chapter Eleven - Theatre	*167*
Chapter Twelve - She Works Hard For The Money	*187*
Chapter Thirteen - Relapse	*204*
Chapter Fourteen - Recovery	*214*
Chapter Fifteen - A Hopeful Ending	*227*
Afterword	*236*

bastardography

xɔːtəcbʌɪˈɒgrəfi/

noun

noun: **bastardography**; plural noun: **bastardographies**
an account of a person's life written by a complete bastard. 'she made herself out to be such a prick in her bastardography'

> 'It is good to love many things, for therein lies the true strength, and whomsoever loves much performs much, and can accomplish much, and what is done in love is well done.'
>
> *Vincent Van Gogh*

> 'I think… if it is true that there are as many minds as there are heads, then there are as many kinds of love as there are hearts.'
>
> *Leo Tolstoy, Anna Karenina*

PREAMBLE

> 'You know, everybody's ignorant, just on different subjects.'
>
> *Will Rogers*

Hello, I'm Simon. Pleased to meet you.

Sorry, I didn't mean to kiss you quite like that, I got a bit carried away, forgive me.

This is a rather mad book about a rather mad person. I wanted to call it *Queer, Creative, Borderline: A Patchwork Memoir*. But I was vetoed. I also wanted to call it *Virgin Detaching a Staircase*, but you can't have everything. The point of the original title was that I wanted to hammer into the name of the book three important masts that are aspects of who I am. Aspects that could be a part of you reading this. And how being queer, having traits of Borderline Personality Disorder, and wanting to create stuff have affected my passage thus far through life. It also documents how I've managed to negotiate with the outside world.

A friend of mine said, 'You're a bit young to be writing a biography, aren't you? You've not really done anything yet,' which worried me, too. But deeper than that, why *am* I writing this book? Well for one, there are no biographies of gay men, or really men of any discernable sexual orientation, that have described their experiences of having a personality disorder, so that may help. Also, I was subjected to a lot of homophobic bullying at school, and books about that are also likely to be good for young LGBTQIA+ people...

Not many books begin with a tract defending their right to exist, but defending one's right to exist is an intrinsic part of who I am. Maybe Katie Hopkins or Michael Gove could try that next time, and see if their defence merits continued living.

The idea of this book has been tossed around for a while. I've always wanted to write a book, though about what I've never been quite sure. The editor asked me for 70,000 words about my life. That was something that immediately made me feel ill. He asked me to write about myself. 'How indulgent!' they'll say. 'How exposing! How embarrassing! How personal!' the family will cry.

I've tried different approaches and it's been written with different voices from different angles, rewrite after rewrite, over the last two years. A lot of the time I wanted to stop or give up. But I didn't, so here it is, finally : The Book.

* * *

Pleasures have never been a simple matter for me. For the longest time, I didn't feel I could experience pleasure. My anxieties were so varied and multitudinous that I destroyed my toys, ruined conversations, and had tantrums at parties.

It's taken a quarter of a century to iron out the kinks, and to turn my corporeal being into a machine that can just about engage confidently with the world. It's been a journey, and one that I'm going to share with you… in a bit. The seeds have always been there. Ever since I could hold a pen, I wrote. Ever since I could process thoughts, even if they were often just an emotional jumble of anxiety, terror and disassociation, I really thought about things and, yes, ever since I could maintain an erection, it was invariably produced by erotic thoughts of the male gender.

I don't want to give away the secret of how I made my life with its various set-backs liveable and inhabitable – that would be silly. It's an accumulation of all the words you've (hopefully) just spent ten quid on, but if you have ADD or are reading this section on Amazon Preview - and let's face it, I've probably told you to download this in the first place, personally - or are in a bookshop without any intention of buying it, or reading the rest - the secret to having a good life is… there is no secret. No, that's cheap; no, the answer is that you have to face your problems and make them work for you. You have to take whatever positive talent (whether it be spiritual, physical or metaphorical) and use that to your advantage. It's that old corny line 'it was there all along', like an anal polyp. You can feel what it is even if you can't see it. But how I got there, and all the misadventure between the womb and Wimbledon Broadway, well, therein lies our tale.

Oh, and remember to live in the present moment! That's important, too.

1.
BIRTH

A Haiku

During Ghostbusters
Mum's waters broke, I was poured
From womb to potty.

'The two most important days in your life are the day you are born and the day you find out why.'

Mark Twain

They used to say they didn't know where I came from. They said they found me under a stone.

I come from an intelligent, hard-working and flawed family. They are funny and self-deprecating by nature, have a fondness for drink and naps in the afternoon, and enjoy the simple pleasures of life.

I know for a fact that they don't want to be written about. In more fanciful moods when they were being very uncouth I said I'd save dishing the dirt on them for my memoirs. But whatever I have ended up disclosing in this book is only the tip of the iceberg. I don't want to intentionally embarrass my nearest and dearest, but I guess I am going to.

What follows is a lifetime of opinions about my dad. It feels naughty to talk about a member of my family so candidly when you, noble reader, don't need to know about him. He is incredibly shy and private (as is my mum) so to have his life summarised in a character bio would certainly induce him to nausea and anger.

He's been a complete cunt for a lot of my life though, so fair's fair…

CHARACTER PROFILES : FATHER

Name: Simon [I know, having the same name is a bone of contention]
Gender: Male (80%), Troll Creature (20%)
Sexual Orientation: I think he would define himself as 'heterosexual', but when pressed in later years, me having discovered his tranny porn stash, he would say that everyone is 'to some degree, bisexual'.
Age: When I was born he was 26 and he is now 54. He will be all these ages and perhaps even younger at points throughout the following tract.
Class/Status: Working Class, was often mistaken for a Bosnian Refugee in the 90s.
Physical Description: Dark olive skin, hair brown, eyes brown, lots of navy tattoos; in later years piercings to the ears, nipples and penis. Wears variants of combat attire.
Quirks: Unresolved PTSD from childhood trauma and serving in the Falklands Conflict.
Morality: Essentially a good man.
Personality Strengths/Weaknesses: Incredibly strong work ethic. Never known to have a sick day, incredible stamina when it comes to strenuous activity, a hidden intelligence, fondness for steam trains/engines, fishing, a great social ability

with other men of similar interests. Ability to grow and change his opinion, to not repeat the horrors perpetrated on him by his father. However, in order to keep his head above water, he has become incredibly selfish and self-interested.

Skills: Driving, survival weekends, fixing engines, fishing.

Education: I remember him mentioning a cookery certificate once.

Likes/Dislikes: Fred Dibnagh, Bear Grylls, Extreme Fishing with Robson Green, The Trooping of the Colour 1971… and as for dislikes, list anything humanity has been responsible for in the last 40,000 years (with the exception of the above).

Childhood/Backstory: Eldest of three, born to an abusive, alcoholic and criminal father (who also beat his mother), he spent most of his time trying to get away from his hostile home environment, finally taking refuge with his grandmother (later known as Nanny 'OOH ARS'), he escaped into the Navy as soon as possible, spending his late adolescence as one part of Her Majesty's Boat Types.

Profession: Mechanic

Relationships: Long Time Partner of Liz, Friends to Skin, Deaf John, Mad Tom, Filthy Eric, estranged from Sister (fat) and Brother (racist), Stepfather to Emz.

Religious Beliefs: None whatsoever. He has the eyes of someone who knows that there is no God.

Fantastical Traits: A sweet and churlish sense of humour.

Goals: To become a blacksmith, to retire, to live comfortably without the stress of the idiots he has been forced to work with.

Skipping the conception (which I am sure was lovely; I wasn't there for the majority of it) and nine months' gestation, I was born in late December 1987 at St. Helier Hospital in South

London. My mother, Elizabeth, went into labour during the network premiere of *Ghostbusters*. The shock of seeing Zool's dog-beast minions rip out of Sigourney Weaver's upholstery made my mum's waters break. She still reminds me that she was peeved she didn't get to see the end.[1]

Also, to add insult to injury, she birthed me into a potty that was given to her as she was straining, bless her. 'Start as you mean to go on', she says now, from behind her glass of cheap Australian Shiraz[2].

As a baby I didn't sleep and would cling to my mother, crying whenever I was put down and left alone. As I grew, I would want to stay with her at every opportunity, often sitting with her and her adult friends rather than play with children my own age. Even then I mistrusted my peer group. The other toddlers simply followed the zeitgeist of marbles and yo-yos. I was so beyond that, and already joining in with conversations about the expansion of the Universe and the FTSE.

I don't know much about my toddling moments, except that we lived in Ambleside Gardens on Brighton Road in Sutton in a small block of flats in a rather non-descript residential area. The only bit of trivia that I can impart is that I grew up a stone's throw from where Quentin Crisp experienced most of his childhood. There must be something in the water!

My first genuine memory is of nursery school.

I was wandering about the classroom, in a world of my

---

[1] But let's be fair, the third act of *Ghostbusters* is hardly cinema's finest hour. The idea of changing Gozer the Destructor from Pee-Wee Herman to 'that prehistoric bitch' was, I feel, ill-judged by Ivan Reitman, the director of *Evolution* and *My Super Ex-Girlfriend*.

[2] Actually, it's probably a Merlot.

own, as the other children were doing, something derivative probably, when suddenly Mrs. Fish demanded that we show our paintings to Santa Claus, who was coming specially from the North Pole to examine our artistry. My heart started to race. I didn't want to let old St. Nick down, coming on such a long flight through many time zones, a man of his great age, and for me to be accused of being selfish and as indolent as to not have contributed to my class gallery.

As the others gathered excitedly to sit in the story-time area, I rushed to the paint pots and coloured card. I dashed the fluorescent canvas with the pigeon-feet splodges of my paintbrush. There were arcs of green and purple across the card. I ran a glue stick haphazardly over the wet paint, and sprinkled sequins over the top. I rushed with my crinkly masterpiece over to the drying rack and slotted it amongst the others' 'work', then joined my comrades.[3]

Santa approved of my efforts, citing the brushstrokes as particularly vibrant with the offset of 'fat glitter'. Could this have been the late Brian Sewell in disguise, searching for artists of the future... Who can say? Although, of course, if this were true, Operation Yewtree would have been contacted.

The 'painting'[4] was kept up on the wall with my fellow nursery-goers' attempts until the end of winter, and it always used to give me a little thrill to see something I had made, captured in a buzzing moment of energy, perfectly still on the wall.

My creativity also ventured into other areas, as with

---

[3] Such procrastination has dogged me to this day.

[4] I preferred the term VISUAL ESSAY, and I am sure Santa Sewell would've agreed with me if he didn't have a ribbon to cut at Thresher's (Alco-eggnog being all the rage in the early nineties; blame John Major)

the creation of two imaginary friends, PeePee and ZeeLee.

The male (if you could define it as possessing a specific gender, but to distinguish it from ZeeLee, we'll say PeePee was male) stood at 11 feet; a translucent tentacle that hovered off the ground. It scrawled and spiralled about behind me, squeaking in a foreign tongue that can only be described as white noise or radio static. PeePee had a very high-pitched squeal. He was my first and only imaginary friend. You could, of course, argue that ZeeLee, his wife and confidante, was my second imaginary friend, but I feel PeePee created her himself to have as a companion when I wasn't around. A spacetime spare rib. Either that or my brain simply couldn't concentrate on him.

The lifespan of an imaginary friend is a precarious concept. Some live only a few months, some for just a day, but others linger in the subconscious forever. Perhaps I died a long time ago and PeePee is at the controls now, making me think these thoughts and type these words.

I was a show-off as a child. That's a fair assumption to make. I was effeminate (we'll get onto that in a bit), gangly and loud. Oh, I was loud. I was prone to illnesses and infections, and my lack of co-ordination meant that a lot of these mystery illnesses coincided with sports days or events. Spooky, that. But to that finger-wagging lot that say with a slight sneer of an innocent little boy that I was a 'show off', I say to them, 'fuck off and die, cunt'... No - joking, joking.[5] I would ascertain that I was simply uninhibited. I didn't even realise I was loud. Often people would wince and recoil at my 3,000 decibels out-of-tune rendition of *Yellow Submarine*, or was it at the fact

---

5   So not joking.

that I was effeminate (again, we'll get onto that in a moment I promise, darlings).

Now, like a prosecuting barrister, I offer up more evidence of my personality and how it formed against my better interest. Exhibit B, which follows, details my pre-pubescent theatrical career.

The first such occasion was in Year Two, when I got to play *The Vicar of Nibbleswicke* for World Book Day. We were all asked to dress up as a character from fiction and my fellow pupils got Mummy and Daddy to pick out *Alice in Wonderland*, *The Hungry Caterpillar* and '*O*' to dress up as. Luckily my parents hadn't ever read a book, so I picked one myself. This tale of a leftfield dyslexic vicar was a short story penned by Roald Dahl[6] to raise money for the Dyslexic Society. A lot of the things he said were scandalous, like 'you must pis your tea', 'krap your cars' and referring to a neighbour's mutt as 'a good little god'. This, of course, when I gave a rendition to my fellow class-mates, resulted in gales of laughter. Oh yes, I was always one to set the table aroar.

I was selected to perform in front of the whole school on that day, and even won £3 in book vouchers. In those days £3 was worth about… well, £3. I couldn't let go of *The Vicar of Nibbleswicke*. Even when my nan picked me up from school, I was blessing the passengers on the 280 bus.

Of course, the vicar performance didn't go unnoticed, and just a few short years later, I was picked to play Willy Wonka in the school assembly, where I had to master the art of a roly-poly, something that required a gym-mat and a lot of patience. I managed it eventually and the juniors were soon

---

6 Beastly anti-Semite.

abuzz with speculatory chatter about my next starring role.[7]

The Year Six play was *The Wizard of Oz*, an amateur play script personally written by Mrs. Woodhouse, the music teacher, which joked about a cyclone tearing through Sutton. What a card!

Auditions were held in the assembly hall at lunchtime, and I offered an entirely improvised piece, where I acted out an episode of *Jerry Springer*, doing all the characters.[8] A risky punt, but it landed me the part of The Scarecrow, and with a slight amendment to the costume (they'd given me a tail, which I hastily ripped off), I was away. My scarecrow acting and prat falling was so convincing, certain audience members were convinced I had an inner-ear infection.

In the last year of junior school my creative juices were really flowing. I'd already written and illustrated a novella entitled *The Return of The Brownie-Blacky Things*,[9] recorded numerous audio stories, penned a long-running newsletter[10] and even composed a topical playlet about my teacher Mr. Fenwick upon his retirement, called *The Mr. Fenwick Leaving Play*. It was a scandalous tale about dear Mr. Fenwick being

7   I hope the sarcasm comes across?

8   I'd had a lot of practice at this point, as some girls in my class and I would use our lunchtime creating sketches and even a full-length puppet show that then went on to take up an entire afternoon, when we performed it in front of our class – SWIVEL ON THAT, NICKY MORGAN!

9   It concerned an alien race TBBT who enslaved The Toothy Pegs after a long feuding war; the resultant invasion by *The Browny-Blacky Things* was put to a stop to by Vic Reeves and Bob Mortimer, who unfortunately came a cropper themselves when confronted by a Cyclops known only as 'One eyed Foo'. Also despite the title being *The Return of...* it was the first and only instalment of the saga. Think *Dune* but more entertaining. I also cringe at the use of the word 'Blacky' now, but at the time I had no knowledge of its less salubrious racist applications.

10 The only subscriber to 'THE SIMON JAY NEWSLETTER' was my grandfather.

replaced by an evil, cold and calculating teacher,[11] The playlet was coached by Mr. De la Parell, our headmaster. Oh, what halcyon days they were.

Here is a recreation of my first written and performed play, which was performed in a Year Six assembly. I discount a variety of pieces prior to this work, such as a puppetry play in Year Five with Vanesha, and other shorter, less considered works such as *Bus Stop,* performed with Thomas P. and my step-cousin Lewis, at the age of 7 or 8, most of which were recreations of Fast Show sketches, and which took place in the living room of Halesowen Road.

SCENE 1

[A school classroom; Two children, Zeena and Zaneb, sit at desks adjacent to one another, heads down, immersed in their school work. Mr. Fenwick enters.]

Mr. Fenwick: Now pupils, pupils… please. Pencils down, boys and girls.

[Zeena and Zaneb applaud wildly]

Mr. Fenwick: Sorry to disturb you whilst you're hard at work creating a more sophisticated standard of material than you're expected to –

---

[11] A very thinly disguised version of our replacement Mrs. Smith, a rancid cow, who, as I now recall, was very personal about yours truly; namely my behaviour, body language and physical appearance. One can only conclude that she was masking some deep sexual attraction… Yes, that's the only explanation.

Zeena: That's alright sir. You inspire us so with your interesting stories and –

Zaneb: - Yes, our work wouldn't be this good without your unorthodox teaching methods.

Mr. Fenwick: Well, that's sweet, but the reason I interrupt is because I am to retire with immediate effect and I want to introduce you to my replacement who, incidentally, I have never met, and who apparently was chosen at random by our headmaster. Pupils, I give you - Mrs. Crabsach.

[Shocked gasps and disappointed groans – Mrs. Crabsach enters, a tiny Chinese woman]

Mr. Fenwick: Well, I best be going, the helicopter is waiting. Toodle-pip!

[Mr. Fenwick exits, Mrs. Crabsach looms over the pupils menacingly]

BLACKOUT.

SCENE 2

[Zeena and Zaneb writing frantically at their desks as Mrs. Crabsach paces up and down – Zeena coughs and Mrs. Crabsach descends on her]

Mrs. Crabsach: How rude… interrupting everyone's work! This is a disgrace! Stand up! Do you hear me? Stand right up

now, in front of everyone. I want everyone to see how much of an insolent waste of space you really are!
[Zeena stands up, shaking]

Mrs. Crabsach: You're a bad, bad girl-child, Zeena! You think you're something special, don't you, showing off in class, with your silly, stupid noises. But I know you. I know your parents!

Zaneb: Please, Mr. Fenwick, please come back and save us from this tyranny!

Mrs. Crabsach: No one's going to save you now, children. You're mine forever!

[She laughs hysterically]

[A crash, followed by sounds of window panes breaking, a brilliant flash of light. The children cheer. Mrs. Crabsach cowers and gasps. Enter Mr. Fenwick in a plume of smoke, now sporting a cape and sword]

Mrs. Crabsach: How NOT nice of you to join us, Fenwick!

Mr. Fenwick: *[Striking heroic pose]* That's Super Fenwick to you! Looks like I got here just in time!

Mrs. Crabsach: You're too late, Fenwick. These pupils' sense of self-worth has been utterly destroyed forever.

Mr. Fenwick: Only whilst your black evil heart pumps its oily poison! *En garde!*

[Mr. Fenwick launches at Mrs. Crabsach who transforms into a giant dragon. Attacking the beast with his sword, Mr. Fenwick shields himself and the children from Crabsach's fire breath. After some choreographed ducking and diving, 'Super Fenwick' delivers his final powered plunge into the dragon's guts with his sword, and the dragon falls, crumpled, to its death. The children whoop and cheer]

BLACKOUT.

Perhaps in my recreation I might have dressed it up a little, but a play very similar to this was performed to my assembly for a real teacher who inspired our class, and especially me. Also he *was* replaced with a very unkind and spiteful teacher. I was subtly warned by some teachers prior to its performance by the repeated leading question, 'This play isn't going to embarrass anybody, is it?' At ten, I feel my satirical bent was at its keenest.

All this concentration on my Juvenalia is because that urge to make and do things was constant. I don't know why, it was just prolific! What eight year old boy would save up all his pocket money for a typewriter? The machine that produced my first novel, which involved organ transplants and strange resurrections of evil flesh tropes (that common one), changed my life.

These were joyous times. Creativity is such a precious thing. It seems something hardwired into human contentment, to be able to reproduce the world through one's own imagination and then manipulate and communicate with it in ways that simple conversation cannot equal. I did lose this zeal at one point. I guess it can dry up if you're not careful. Yes, a happy creative childhood in that respect.

When I was seven, I used to go around the classroom and kiss all the boys on the lips, and say, 'I'm going to marry each and every one of you', not quite grasping the then one dimensional aspect of marriage. It didn't strike me as particularly odd that I liked boys and that one day I'd be opening an antiques shop with a man named Miguel, and owning a small dog. It wasn't until there appeared a large amount of opposition from the fellow bastards in my class, and the teachers, and their parents (the children's parents - I didn't meet any of the parents of the teachers, so their views about gay people is anyone's guess) that I again tried to hide my true feelings.[12]

I knew what I was before I could put a name to it. I remember being a tiny little thing, going all doe-eyed at the boys on *Home and Away* with their beach-buff bodies; thinking how resourceful handbags were as a utility in which to carry one's walkie-talkie and sweets. I used to de-robe my action men and paint them brown with a felt-tip pen. Hot! But the clincher was happening upon these little pictures of naked men, hidden away in a box in my parents' bedroom.[13] They must have been culled from the 80s, all bearded and hairy, with big circumcised willies. I remember, even at 8, getting an erection, not that I want you necessarily to imagine my pre-pubescent rod, but... yes, that's what happened.

It was giggly and fun, and naughty, but I knew deep

12 This suppression of truth seems to be a bit of a recurring theme.

13 Thus, at the age of seven, began my lifelong love of pornography. Actually let's call it erotica, because 'porn' is a politicised word and conjures up images of creampied eighteen year olds in school uniforms – yucky! I mean the arty Mapplethorpe type stuff.

down this had to be a secret, a total secret. All the tickling and endless hugging of other boys at school, one couldn't let on that there was anything nicer about it than just being innocent boyish fun…

Oh I had crushes, a million crushes, before my age got to double digits. There was the boy who would've been in Year Six when I was in Year Four, who always used to look after me in the playground. When my U.F.O. *Unexplained* Fil-o-fax got ripped up and scattered over the asphalt of our play-area by some mean children, he spent the rest of lunch helping me put it back together. Even though my mother is a hardcore atheist, she was close friends with an eccentric Christian known only as Jackie, who thought it would be a good idea to let me go on a Christian retreat week in Morden.[14] It was at this Christian Camp at the age of 9, that I fell in love with a man for the first time; the deep true love of a child, unconditional and unfettered. It felt like he was a man to me, but he was probably just 17. Very well spoken, with big green eyes and that wiry, sprightly cheery disposition of someone who is resilient about life and all that it entails. That's what happens when you have Jesus for a sunbeam, I guess. I always managed to make him laugh with jokes about breast enlargements that went wrong and other such punning linguistic delights, to which he complimented me no end: 'You're so clever, Simon, you're so witty, Simon, you're such a great guy…', he would always say to me. Oh, how I loved him.

14 This was after the failed Sunday school sessions where I asked the 'teachers' why children in the 'Third World' were allowed to starve and that only a cruel and unintelligent God would create beings just to see them die by his own negligence. If God was a person, he'd be like that woman who was done for Baby P... I didn't say that as it hadn't happened then, but that was how forthright my analogy was and why I wasn't allowed back to Sunday school.

It was when we got to the precipice of 'Big School' and all it involved, that some of the boys made their position on sexuality very clear. One in particular, Reiss, was exceptionally homophobic, and went on about wanting to lock gay people in the cellar and 'cure' them. Some other children wanted to go 'gay-busting', and they victimised one boy, who obviously had learning difficulties. Because he didn't understand what 'gay' meant, he agreed when they asked him if he was, and I, of course went along with this, as I had no idea of what else to do.[15]

Perhaps it's been a staple of bullying for a long time, but I really felt a surge of 'you're gay' meant the worst kind of insult around. At this time, 'gay' was shorthand for everything that was the lowest, vilest, and most despicable of things. Surely this was transmitting into every LGBTQIA+ child in our school, and yet no one did anything about it. I hope the parents and teachers that presided over perhaps the last generation of children to feel entirely guilty and left-out just because of who they happened to be are ashamed of themselves, but perhaps I am churlish to think this will be the last generation to feel like that. Nevertheless there'll be plenty of time for accusations later. I won't disappoint.

In terms of my own gayness, not only was my burgeoning sexuality pointing towards the man on man, but the benefits of having an older sister with *Teengirl* mags containing Hollyoaks hunk centrefolds was a huge help. I also, through no fault of my own, had developed the mannerisms and behaviour ascribed to the stereotype of gay boys. I crossed my legs like a girl. I was very delicate, I had an effeminate voice that lilted and elongated with classic emphatic dips in

---

[15] The old SS guard 'They told us there were jobs' Nuremberg Trial excuse.

my sentences. I was mocked[16] for my ways and told to not 'do it' so much. I could see the utter fear in my father's eyes. He was very homophobic at the time[17], and would warn me that the idea of becoming gay would result in me having to insert tampons into my anus to soak up the blood that would haemorrhage from it after some (obviously rough, unprotected and loveless) violation. The problem was that acting like the precocious child I wanted to be, I'd pretend to take this all in my stride and feign a knowing, 'Oh I know exactly what you're talking about' face, when I actually had no idea what semen was until I was fifteen.

As a postscript I find it amusing that, years later, I had to defend my dad and vouch for his disposition as a tolerant libertarian after he almost lost his job for making homophobic comments at work. I had to write a statement of support to his managers. This is it:

'My father has always supported my work, not only emotionally and financially where he can, but in his offering of advice and the keen insight into my creative process that he regularly provides.

Having worked in the theatre since University in 2008, he has come to see me in plays in which I have worked with my boyfriend. He has also made sizable donations to our joint theatre efforts, not only in Bournemouth, but also London and Edinburgh. This year the artistic director of LGBTQIA+ Freedom To Be has kindly made me Resident Director, after two of my projects, the second being *Queer Macbeth*, had been

---

16 Perhaps very slightly, to family members reeling at this, going 'We never mocked you' in 'holier than thou' guilty tones...

17 As of 2016, he is practically Peter Tatchell when it comes to gay rights – ha!

staged through the LGBTQIA+ Freedom To Be festival. My father knows how important LGBTQIA+ activism is to me, having witnessed the emotional and physical traumas I had to suffer when I was a victim of sustained homophobic bullying at school, which in turn led to a nervous breakdown.

My father supported me throughout this time by talking to psychiatrists, schoolteachers and doctors with my mother, and was always pressing for more to be done to counteract the experiences I had suffered. It's with his support that I have managed to gain the confidence necessary to pursue a career in the theatre, and do charity work through Stonewall and LGBTQIA+ Freedom To Be. I am forever indebted to him for that support.'

2.
POCAHONTAS

'I have been told by my publisher's solicitor that using the quotation I had chosen for this chapter would be like writing an elaborate suicide note if I were to insert it, so in the interests of remaining alive, I hereby forego its inclusion in my magnum opus.'

A significant religious book, somewhere in the world

Whenever it comes up in conversation now, the fact for my parents that the alarm bells didn't ring off the hook from an early age is put down to 'we thought you might be dyslexic, autistic' and so on – without much of a follow-up.

I was a sensitive and effeminate child[18] who didn't sleep very well. I was always self-conscious of my 'self', and from as soon as I can recall, my brain would rush to anxiety and terror at the slightest provocation.

The dizzying *déjà vu* of realising that one existed at all was such an overwhelming concept that it caused me to panic even before I could give it a name. The fear would take me over, and I would rush to my mother, whereupon she'd say something like, 'Gosh, your heart's beating so fast, Simon. What on earth's the matter?', to which I could say nothing.

When I found out I was going to die one day, death

---

[18] 'You've said effeminate like a hundred fucking times already, Si... We get it,' you say. Well, I say 'don't use 'like' in a sentence' and it *wasn't* a hundred times, it was, like, just a few times... oh shit...

was explained to me by my mother as 'you die and there is nothing forever'. This didn't sit too well, and I was immediately triggered into a panic attack. Then again I could be triggered by the slightest thing. A famous example is the time I screamed my head off during the cinema screening of *Pocahontas*.

I would like to take this opportunity to apologise to the patrons in Screen Two of the Sutton UCI on June 26th 1995. It was during the Disney film *Pocahontas,* described by Roger Ebert as 'ha[ving] a lot of good intentions, but a severe scoundrel shortage', that I had my first major panic attack. I was seven. It was a panic attack (for the lack of a better term, it will have to be described as such), that would become legendary in my home as a child, and cause me much embarrassment. A lot of the strange things I did as a child, like having panic attacks, dressing up in girls' clothes and trying to choke myself with pencils, were often repeated at the Sunday dinner table for comic effect. But it was my 'outburst' in the cinema which stood the test of time. This moment also chronicled the first of my screaming fits. This was a perfect example of how I'd succumb to such a state.

We were sitting in the cinema happily watching the film, and, for some reason, perhaps it was something that was happening on screen, I distinctly recall Pocahontas jumping off a cliff. I've been so traumatised about the film that I've never seen it since. I'm convinced it was something in my mind. I was an introverted child, my thoughts were constantly racing and reality always seemed an unbelievable and unnecessary construct. I also have the sneaking suspicion that *Pocahontas* bored the arse off me. So, in any case, my thoughts were wandering, and they soon happened upon the subject of Death. My mind had the canny knack of being able to tell me that my corporeal being would simply cease, and that I'd be nothing, zilch, nada, for all eternity, and I could actually feel the concept of eternity draining the life-force from my cells. I was basically a Damien Hirst formaldehyde shark in a tank! As these thoughts of the eternal nothingness took over my mind like a nightmarish translucent jellyfish, my entire being flipped out, and a dangerous amount of adrenaline shot through my tiny frame. The fight or flight mechanism was triggered and the glut of terrified energy would have to somehow find a means of escape. I have no shame in telling you that even writing about it now in 2016 is causing a slight ripple of that adrenaline to course through me… Luckily I can now control it… almost!

In this first instance of this happening, my larynx contracted and I screamed, 'Shit, Fuck, Shit, Bollocks, I Don't Want To Die, I Don't Want To Die!' and bit my mother's tit as hard as I could, before flailing my limbs all over the place.

I was taken to the foyer by my parents, sobbing, my entire body trembling. In the aftermath, I was simply deeply embarrassed, as my mum tried to comfort me, and my dad looked on, horrified.

This was only the beginning, as these 'fits' would continue with varying frequency up until late adolescence. As did wetting the bed. I wonder if the two are connected? Before I get onto that subject, I want to stay with the theme of the death panics or 'Freak Outs' as my dad affectionately called them.

I used to have these panics every so often, until I got to the point where I could hide them, round about my early teens, ditto the existentialist panics, which usually happened around bedtime. Consequently I became an insomniac, and when it all got too much for me, I'd have a fit, which would make me do strange things like force a pencil down my throat, or bite deep into my finger so the bone became exposed.

All of this unpleasantness coupled with the paranoid feeling of 'why am I me?' saw me as self-absorbed as I could be. I felt the fact that only I could see out of my own eyes, meant that I had some special secret that no-one had told me about. Perhaps the rest of reality was a fiction, or some horrible Truman Show / Franz Kafka fuck-up, which was providing the setting for my life. All of this was far too much for a boy who still watched *Live and Kicking* whilst munching Coco Pops on a Saturday morning. All I had been taught had me conclude that I should bear down with these prickly terrors and just try to pretend that everything happening in front of my eyes wasn't actually happening.

Bad move, dear, but I guess the only one you could've made in the circumstances.

Another detail, or jigsaw piece if you will, was the newly discovered propensity to be miserable, detached, to complain of feeling lonely, sad or that I didn't fit in with the others. All those times I spent staring out of the window, watching the other kids play, crying on the way to school, or begging mother to not go in, meant I could hardly bear another day of sitting on my own at lunchtime. Some of this was diva-ish and a cry for attention, but more often than not I was genuinely heartbroken. Something was missing and sad inside me. It was deep and pain-filled. Perhaps the reason other children didn't want to play with me was that I sometimes pissed the bed, and to avoid the awkward confrontation with mum (or worse, dad) I simply 'pretended it hadn't happened', and went in, reeking of urine.

In Year Five, the teacher I had was from Newcastle.

I can't remember her name, so let's call her Mrs. Northern, though I doubt anyone would've been stupid / blind / masochistic enough to actually marry the whore. Anyway, she took a bit of a shine to me,[19] and even called in my parents to say, 'Simon seems a bit down. Anything wrong at home?' All that kind of nonsense, the stuff that councils and social workers are usually negligent about when it comes to the need to provide care. However, her assumption that I was being knocked about, or knocked off, was completely unfounded. In the end, I was just a child who was a grizzly grumpy Gus. And like all people who keep an eye on the depressed, she got bored and annoyed, and finally ended up regularly complaining whenever I looked sad, or cried, and huffed, 'Oh no, not again! If you complain once more, I'm going to send you to Mrs. Southern'.[20]

Another memory that sticks in my mind that can't be recalibrated to sweetness, is that of my aunt and uncle sitting one day discussing what I was going to be when I grew up. I was, of course, sitting watching them from the corner, aged probably about six. They said that I could be an astronaut, or a doctor, or a fireman, with dutiful jokes about my perceived flaws[21] in tow. But at some dying point of the conversation, my aunt said, 'Perhaps he'll be [does limp wrist motion]', and my uncle retorted, 'Yes I think he'll definitely be [does limp wrist motion]'. They laughed and looked at me. I demanded to know what they meant. Of course, they kept their secret

19 Not in a 'Paedo Mrs. Smith' kind of way.

20 Think Hitler in a flowery blouse, wearing rubber gloves.

21 On top of being loud, my other cardinal sin was that I spoke far too much for their liking, and out of turn to boot, which was a double whammy for a human being, to make their feelings known... Gosh, what a terrible cunt of a child I was for speaking... Why didn't they sew my mouth shut, silly fat relatives... tsk!

hand signals a mystery.

I knew, however, that the person I was going to be would make a lot of people laugh.

Despite what I've written above, and especially immediately above, my grandparents' house was always a place that was filled with laughter, with lots of quoting *Monty Python*, *Fawlty Towers* and ruder things like *Crapston Villas* by my aunt and uncle. They were quite a pair back in the day. Look at me almost apologising for dobbing them in… This is the problem when some of your family remain alive and literate.

3.
MADNESS FOREPLAY

'About a third of my cases are suffering from no clinically definable neurosis, but from the senselessness and emptiness of their lives. This can be defined as the general neurosis of our times.'

Carl Jung

My Head of Year took an interest in my 'problematic behaviour'. It was only when I was in secondary school and had a terrible and inexplicable bout of psoriasis that covered my entire body bar the face, that some psychiatric intervention was sought in the form of Dr. Dinnick, via our family G.P. .

YOUR OPINION ON THIS BOY

S D C HELLMAN
HEALTH CENTRE
ROBIN HOOD LANE
SUTTON

DR. BURP

SUTTON GENERAL HOSPITAL

19.03.02

I would be most grateful for your opinion on this boy, who recently came to see me with his mother. I have enclosed a photocopy of some bullet points made with the counsellor he has been seeing at school. It is a good summary of his feelings and the problems he is encountering. I saw him yesterday, and he was fairly articulate about his problems, and struck me as an intense, anxious young man, who was rather withdrawn and is now socially isolated from his peers. Unfortunately, over the last couple of months, counselling at school has produced no obvious behavioural improvement or change in his general attitude towards school, his peer group, and his rather negative feelings about the future. There was some confusion between his mother and himself about how long this had probably been going on, but it would appear to have been deteriorating gradually over the last year. I would value your opinion on his further management.

Yours sincerely

S D C HELLMAN

It has been suggested that Simon see a G.P. with the intention of seeking a referral to a psychologist or psychiatrist. This has come out of concerns regarding many of the things Simon is experiencing. These include:

- *A constant feeling of negativity.*
- *Simon described never feeling happy, even when laughing or appearing happy.*
- *Feels pressure to live up to other people's expectations.*
- *Fear of being in the spotlight or standing out in any way.*

- *Constant worrying before, during and after events.*
- *Obsessive thoughts.*
- *Hypervigilance.*
- *Difficulty sleeping – worrying thoughts before sleeping, needs to be distracted by radio… etc.*
- *General feeling of unenthusiasm – constantly feels let down, rarely excited.*
- *Feels it is a struggle to get through the school day.*
- *Constantly feels tired and lethargic.*

My parents didn't like family therapy and continued to complain about our psychiatrist's facial twitch. The upshot of my psychiatric exploration was that I continued to be prescribed Seroxat[22] for anxiety and depression, which in turn finally caused me to become manic and convinced that any van passing the house was a van for me, and a van that was coming to take me away. I was, in fact, taken off shortly afterwards.

I was always 'sensitive'.

I don't like that word.

It denotes several things about my character, specifically traits that I still haven't entirely got to grips with.

Now you'll have to bear with me, because I do tend to ramble, and with the genesis of all that has transpired and occurred in the complex blur of my adolescence it is a little messy, as life has the tendency to be.

By the time I had reached the second year at my secondary school, a rather rough all boys' state school in a less than reputable area in south London, I realised that I did

[22] Since discontinued for under-eighteens as it caused intense suicidal ideation and a high number of suicides in teenagers and children.

not fit in. The whole ethos of the school was to be fit, healthy and happy 'lads' (I spit that word), who played lots of sport, mucked around with car engines, welded sheets of metal together and hacked bits of wood up to try and make shelves. Despite this, through no obvious design of my own, I was an accidental and annoying cliché, the fay little boy who liked playing with dolls and reading books. You can still tumble into stereotypes even if you don't want to.

I soon made a few friends, and was doing okay academically, and my home life was bearable. I was nevertheless desperately unhappy and preoccupied with obsessional thoughts that were deeply troubling. Negative, dark and destructive, and all irrational, which gave me severe anxiety. I had absolutely no self-esteem. I couldn't sleep at night because I'd inadvertently have panic attacks. As I have already outlined, I wasn't a well boy.

Erratic behaviour and sporadic outbursts of anger followed by long bouts of depression are not uncommon in teenagers, and I think my parents could see I was overwhelmed by this unstable barrage of emotional turmoil. My mother took me to my G.P. and described how I was acting. All I could remember was that I used to sit in the living-room at 3am, dressed and ready for school, miserable, and would argue and shout at my parents a lot. I even used to hit out at them when I was really tired.

The upshot of all this was that I was referred for 'Family Therapy' at the Child and Adolescent Community Mental Health Team.

This did not help.

My parents didn't like sitting in a room with me and the middle-aged woman with the stained floral dress, sandals and a prominent facial twitch, masquerading as a psychiatrist. They were forced to give lengthy rambling confessional answers about how I was treated at home and how I had behaved as a child and how my dad had more or less ignored me all my life. My mother, my constant companion, and my sister, who was actually only my half-sister, managed to cover up, amongst other things, just how obsessed about things and 'sensitive' I was.

Eventually my dear ma and pa were herded out of the room, so 'Twitch', as her nickname became, could have a quiet word. She asked me how I felt and other questions that would become the standard patter for all shrinks over the next seven years and then, finally, she dropped the bomb-shell. She squeaked this odd little string of words in an awkward, guarded, and almost embarrassed way.

'So, do you like boys or do you like girls?'

I knew I was gay, but I didn't think anyone else would, and the fact that I could still push all the thoughts I had to the back of my head so they didn't bother me at all made me stupidly believe I'd got away with it.

At that point I worried that I was going to go red, and just managed to evade the question, with some pretentious intellectualised guff like, 'Oh I don't really think of it in terms of who I would like, but in the terms of who I'd fall in love with, and there are no rules to that. I'd like a person for their personality, not their gender.' All complete bollocks, but thankfully she didn't pursue the subject after that.

We had several more sessions with 'Twitch' until she prescribed me Seroxat, and asked to see us again in three months. As I am sure you are all aware, Seroxat more or less failed as a viable anti-depressant for teenagers after a high proportion of its users ended up trying to die by suicide. Nice.

As I have a terrible fear of death and dying, the Seroxat only seemed to make me paranoid to the point of psychotic delusion, where I became convinced that people were coming to take me away in a van, and that I was going to be experimented on. I became even more fraught and angst-ridden. Good job!

I finally stopped taking Seroxat, and continued to have occasional sessions with 'Twitch' throughout the year.

I wish we'd kept up the family therapy, mainly for my father's sake. For a man with undiagnosed post-traumatic stress disorder, self-medicated with alcohol and cannabis, perhaps Dr. Twitch-face could have doled out a few pills, or even dealt with my mother's tendency to become withdrawn, but hey ho...

These sessions were strange. I've often come to the conclusion that therapy only works when you're well. Paradox? Oxymoron? We need to keep our minds healthy, rather than wait until they fall apart. If only CBT was on the National Curriculum. Or did Gove do away with that?

As puberty loomed, like my apprehension about death and existence, the fear of my sexuality started to creep in, and like the other two big red horrors, the gayness was pushed down into the deep dark secret place, too.

For my sins, I have always liked to expose the truth, or what I perceive to be the truth, whether it puts me in a bad light or not, and in my diaries from the age of about twelve onwards, I was always trying to tell my diary that I was gay. I just couldn't bring myself to write the words on the paper.

Once I'd actually put it down, it would confirm it, cement it, make it true. But for the moment I was just holding back the tide temporarily, like a slightly more successful King Cnut.

4.
SCHOOL OUTING

'I cannot fix on the hour, or the spot, or the look, or the words, which laid the foundation. It is too long ago. I was in the middle before I knew that I had begun.'

Jane Austen, Pride and Prejudice

There's something in John Boorman's *Hope and Glory* about Rosehill Avenue. About it not having roses or hills, or even being an avenue. And that it has no fucking trees!

Perhaps it's the nicest thing anyone has ever said about Rosehill, if people should ever care to mention this fistula hanging off the end of Sutton, Surrey, infecting its slow passage into the urethra of Merton. But for me and my family, it was the setting for nearly a decade of domestic bliss. I mean, of course, blister. For Rosehill was, is and perhaps forever shall be, a cesspool of shit and dull horror. For everything from the dank grey Belsen-like St. Helier Hospital right down to its stretching endless bypass lined by burnt out petrol stations and scenes of regular RTAs, it's a shit tip. Perhaps my experience was soured, but I'll give you a little kiss on the cheek if you can find me someone who has something nice to say about Rosehill. At the time, of course, I didn't know this. Like the people of North Korea who are continually told that there is Nowhere Better On Earth, if all you know is Rosehill, you think the misery it engenders is simply the default state for life.

My sister puts it most effectively: 'We weren't cut out for the estate. We were sweet and innocent.' It is true that we were waif and callow, moving on from Ambleside Gardens a few miles down the road.

I remember the first summer on Halesowen Road, where I innocently tottered out with a big bowl for a water fight, and some fat older girl with the hatred of her mother in her eyes, booted me up the arse and stole my bowl, parading it around brazenly for the rest of the day. My cheeks, face and bum, burned red at the injustice that her crime had gone unpunished. What's life but a fat girl's boot kicking you up the arse repeatedly for all time? It provides the perfect metaphorical description of that time of my life.

On the subject of arseholes, time to talk about secondary school. Yay! The school everyone wanted to go to after the relative bliss of Damaged Primary School was Overly Grunge, a brand spanking new mixed school with multi-coloured lockers and gleaming floors. I went to the Open Day with my mum and was embarrassed by the fact that Laura, who played the Cowardly Lion (badly) alongside my Scarecrow in *The Wizard of Oz*, Year Six, asked after my snake Sammy, a lie I'd obviously told all and sundry a few weeks earlier. I said, 'Oh yes, fine,' to which my mother furrowed her brow.

'What are you talking about, what snake?'

Laura and her mum both gave me a puzzled, disappointed look, and moved on. I used to just talk such lies, from saying both my parents were dead or that I was adopted, or fostered, that I had cancer, was drunk, that my father was black, or that I came from Spain. I sometimes contradicted myself within the space of the same story. I was a walking talking bible, chapter and verse, mouthing utter crap that I almost believed myself as I was saying it.

'Overly Grunge' seemed like a nice school, although I can't say I'd be any happier or that the events that subsequently transpired wouldn't have occurred in some other way had I gone there, not unlike austerity measures improving the economy. You can't compare whether doing nothing would've worked either, if you follow my drift. But in the end, I didn't go to Overly, for the sole reason that my 'best friend' at the time, Michael, said 'Don't go to Overly Grunge, Overly is for losers. You'll want to come to Carslake Boys with me. Won't you Simon?'

I offered a reply that went along the lines of, 'Oh, I'd rather like to go to Overly actually,' to which he just shook his head condescendingly as if I'd just blown a raspberry and simultaneously shat my pants. When you're ten it's hard to argue with friends who will withhold their friendship if you disagree with them. So, under peer pressure from Michael, I relented and put Carslake Boys down as my first choice.

We weren't even in the same house when the time to go to new school came round. I was in Holst, and forced to wear a double yellow striped tie. I was pissed off as the other boys all got a different colour, red or green or even the coveted blue stripe alongside the regulation yellow.

We had been shown round Carslake Boys on their Open Day like dignitaries at the 1936 Berlin Olympics, witnessing the outside splendour of their new Tech Blocks and Grand Assembly Halls. The reality, however, was soon apparent. Grey concrete playgrounds with a mesh fence called 'The Cage' for the Year Sevens. Perhaps this was to protect us, though it all felt a little grim.

During my first day of 'Big School' I got completely

lost on the way to registration. For some reason we found ourselves in the huge green playing field over the way, when I thought we were supposed to be in the science department. I was soon cornered by that churning in the stomach and irritable tingling in the penis that accompanies the fear of being in the wrong place at the wrong time. Luckily another boy, Harrison, also got totally lost, and sweetly we teamed up, talking together in nervous camaraderie until we found our respective groups.

Being late to registration and then again for lunch meant I had to join the first group on the playing field. I couldn't see my friend Michael anywhere and for some reason I got chatting to an obese boy called Leonard. He was just a pile of fat with a boy's face crudely drawn on top, who was excitedly chatting with his new-found friends Peter, a diminutive boy who had a slightly bigger than average head, sort of Gollum-looking, and another boy, Ashcora, a mixed-race young Eric Morecambe, if you can imagine such a thing. Easy, isn't it? Ash was munching a pear, so in my infinite wisdom I called him 'Pear Guy', a nickname that stuck. We were a quartet of freaks that fitted snugly together.

During our morning queues for assembly and uniform checks - 'tighten that tie, tuck in that shirt, you look like a disgrace' - I felt compelled to stand with Michael, although his mocking tones of 'You're embarrassing, you're so annoying' began to grate and I soon wanted to spend less and less time with him. In the end I just ignored him altogether. This has become something of a trait over the years when I stop being people's friends, to varying degrees of success and contentment, even intervention from other mutual friends. 'He's changed, be friends with him. He thinks you're irritating, but you can still be friends' was what the go-between once said. How can anyone refuse an offer like that?

I finally settled into 'Big School', and the routine of my life on the cusp of puberty was standard. Up early, possibly might've wet the bed (still) would wash (maybe) and put on the uniform. I loved the uniform. A blazer. A blazer made me so happy. I'd take breakfast with Mother who, if not premenstrual, would converse on topics as far ranging as string theory to cogitations on various types of arachnid. If she was on, my 'whiny behaviour' might warrant me a hairdryer across the table aimed at my chest, or having my tie 'peanutted' as they used to call it back in the day.

I'd have fun with Leonard, Peter and Ashcora before school and during the lunch and break times. We all shared a similar sense of humour and would quote *The Simpsons* or make up our own surreal anecdotes and ideas. Lessons went okay. I excelled in English, RE and even Maths, being placed in top sets. Everything else I was alright at, except PE and 'Games'. Yes, annoyingly, I lived up to the stereotype.[23] I hated competitive sports. I would run from the ball in rugby, and try to look busy running up and down the sidelines.

Bizarrely, despite my profound lack of sporting prowess, the captain of the football team took an interest in me at one point. He was an obsessive fan of 'The Krays" biopic with the Kemp brothers (especially the gay kiss), and when we used to play about on chat rooms talking to people, he always wanted us to pretend to be women to get men to expose themselves to us. Thinking back on that, these might have been early missed signals.

---

23 I'm not too worried about being seen as a stereotype now, or even then, except for the fact that it does tend to get one into a spot of bother at times.

So, yes, my day consisted of that kind of thing, and then I'd often stay at After School Club where you could sit in a classroom and do what you liked. I used to chat to a cool Scouse boy with terrible teeth; they were dark yellow, a thick film of mustard decay across the molars. Francis Bacon would've killed to have had the chance to paint them. I used this After School Club to write in a journal. By then I was on the second obsessive volume of *Simon's Bits 'n' Bobs* a daily log of thoughts and ideas that I detailed in microscopic script (sticking in pictures and doing collages). I also used this time to plan short films that I wanted to make.

I had got a home movie camera the previous year which I made short films with. The first was called *The Weedkiller* which starred Michael, and involved a man needing his garden landscaped. He has a premonition that he'll be killed by a gardener, although pays it no heed, but in the end he gets killed. Riveting stuff. I even premiered a short film during a geography lesson, *Evil Dead 4*. Making films was how I spent a lot of my evenings when not doing homework. I'd film everything: myself, my family, sketches with my 'cousin' Lewis or friend Adam (who did get to go to Overly Grunge). I had no ability to edit, so I had to film sequentially with diegetic sound effects, and all that. It was unknowingly *Dogme 95* but less shit. Later on I used the same video camera to perform slightly more erotic acts – which makes me think, if I owned such videos of myself at thirteen now, would it be illegal even if they were all of me? It's academic though, because I chucked all my tapes when I left Rosehill.

Home life was quiet. Dad was silent. He'd sit in the corner reading magazines. Stupidly, I tried to look at what he was reading, and he eventually said, ominously, 'Don't look at that, it's got pictures of naked women in,' and snatched it away from me. Mum would watch sitcoms with me such as *Red Dwarf*, *The Brittas Empire*, *Keeping Up Appearances*, *The League of Gentlemen* and *Little Britain*. They were the happiest moments at home. My sister was fifteen and rarely about, hanging out with girls (and boys) from Glenthorne, much to my Father's dismay. He would warn her of STIs and getting stabbed by heroin addicts if she was out beyond 7.30 at night.

The furthest we went from Rosehill round that time was to Gander Green Lane in West Sutton to see my maternal grandparents, a wonderful haven of joy, where the family would gather for Sunday lunch. There was always an atmosphere of family insanity, alcoholism and personality disorders brimming under the surface, but that's for later. I was barely eleven and couldn't see any of that.

Even though I attended an all boys school whose ethos was based on creating Masculine Well-Rounded Men, with a Joy For Sport and a Healthy Disgust Of Women, I was pretty much spared from bullying in my first few years at the school. I was regarded as a nobody and generally ignored. I was called 'gay' and 'faggot' but that was just a standard title given to all boys. It wasn't significantly directed at me yet. I occasionally got picked on but it was more in a tired 'look at how pathetic you are' kind of way. I was far too much in my own head to notice even if it had occurred.

As the years rolled by and puberty kicked in, my diaries became more detailed. Discovering I could masturbate came as a bit of a shock. I think I must have been twelve or thirteen. I remember the moment distinctly, as I was reading Jacqueline Wilson's Double Act (Oh how I adored her books) in bed and just casually twanging my boner under the sheets (as kids do) and I think the twanging went more vertical than horizontal and before I knew it an extreme throbbing came from the base of my cock... I was terrified. I hid under the bedsheets from my own orgasm. It was dry and shocking, but that was all. Now why have I just shared that? There was a reason. I am sure I will remember it. Perhaps it's a watershed moment to mark the onset of puberty, and, in any case, I like the juxtaposition between orgasms and Jacqueline Wilson. It also strikes me as an amusing curiosity for one's sexual awakening to not be about anything sexual. I didn't link it to anything erotic.

In the annals of my own narrative it has sometimes been established that the onset of my mental health problems is intertwined with my 'troubles at school', though this isn't true. They both occurred simultaneously, but one didn't really have that much to do with the other. They ran alongside each other like rail tracks, which makes it hard for me now to write about both simultaneously. Having just said that, my coming out, as in all comings out, was a protracted experience. You come out to people individually. The first person I came out to was my Connexions PA. I had been assigned one by my Head of Year, Mr. Mudguard, because I had experienced difficulty sleeping. He thought it would help me having someone to speak to, though they overlooked the fact that it's not talking I have a problem with. My Personal Advisor, whose role was really to provide careers guidance and stuff like that, was a soft-spoken lovely bucktoothed, fat-arsed antipodean called Gina who only ever got cross with me once. I'd talk to her about everything from death to philosophy and people and school, to obscure comedy. It was around this time I started hinting in my diary, 'I need to tell you something', 'I must say something'... I knew I was gay, but I couldn't bear to write the word. I couldn't acknowledge the physical letters. The fear would consume me if it came to the surface so I had to keep pushing it back down into the depths.

Oddly, my subconscious and the worries of others fed into my protracted outing. I think even though I was a compulsive liar and fantasist, I had and still have a strong streak of honesty, righteousness and the determination to call a spade a spade.[24] I remember members of my family often commenting on my effeminacy in a combined tone of worry and amusement. Obviously I now know that this was down to my (predominately) female family's self-loathing and fear of feminine and womanly things in general. The measure of self-esteem in our family could be comfortably accommodated on the Vatican's abortion clinic register. But then, the idea of being girly was 'gay' or 'weak'. These accusations of 'weakness' and 'unmanliness' plagued me throughout childhood.

To be 'gay' was seen as something terrible. Everyone from my dad, to people at primary school, teachers, librarians, government ministers and even The Archbishop of Canterbury had problems with the concept. So any outlet of gayness when I was younger became confined to private jokes. I have the oddest memories of being at a drag-race with Adam (a boy whose mum was like the one out of *What's Eating Gilbert Grape?*) at about twelve when I said I'd learnt from a drama book about 'how to act gay' and it involved tapping someone else on the knee in an extravagant way. He responded with condescending twattery which seems to be a trait of all my childhood male friends. This was a bit rich seeing as he dry-humped me through my sleeping bag once. I don't want it to look like I'm hating on all

---

24 and for clichés, evidently.

my childhood friends. I had lots of nice friends too. Rashmi and Vanesha are two girls that stick out happily in my memory. Vanesha's dad ran a corner shop and I always got to pick any sweet I liked when we dropped her off from my house and, hang on, I was talking about my coming out, wasn't I? Got a bit sidetracked there.

Yes, Gina, her! She was the first in my memory. It had to be teased out of me, or perhaps I teased it out of myself. I kept saying, 'There is something I really need to tell you'. I managed to get a book out of the then glorious Sutton Public Library called *The Milkman's on His Way* by David Rees, which I've just discovered was published in 1982. What made me laugh was that Gina said, 'If you can't tell me, why you don't you draw me a picture?' I don't know what I would have drawn, but I showed her the blurb of the book and it was done. I can't really remember how she reacted. It was certainly neutral. I didn't really know what to expect. It's odd to think that now I'd have access to internet resources, Stonewall, gay characters on TV, and so on, but then I had to sort of make it up as I went along.

Once I told Gina, I felt more confident about myself. It felt normal. It was even exciting that there was this part of myself that had been submerged, forcibly coming to the fore. I then told Peter (Gollum) on a day out to *Chessington World of Adventures*. He sort of nodded at this and nothing more was said as we enjoyed the log flume and Rameses Revenge, although when I brought it up again later on, he revealed he hadn't really twigged about what I had told him. He was always a little dim.

Being truthful about an aspect of myself really gave me confidence. I felt good. Being open about yourself, whether it's your sexual orientation or your favourite book, is always likely to make you feel better. I've never really thought about it like that before. I think that's the main argument when people say, 'Why come out so young at school? Wait until you're older and there's not so much stigma.' To that I say, 'Fuck off, you utter cunt!'

It's the same as people who say, 'Oh it's not so important. Why go on about it?' To them I say, 'Fuck right off and die, you cunt!' It's tiring to still have to listen to these questions. 'Going on about it' is simply doing what any straight person would do without even thinking. I'm not going to dignify it with further explanation. If you're still reading at this point I doubt I will have to challenge your internalised homophobia. Nevertheless the answer to the first question I'm still only really examining more than a decade after the fact.

And come out I did. This was at the beginning of Year Ten, so I am by now about fourteen. I felt buoyant and confident, like a razor-cheekboned *bon vivant*. I felt mature and wise beyond my years.

All tosh, but I must've had some sort of manic self-belief one particular morning when we were in History and studying the rise of Fascism in 1930s Europe. For some reason, the skinhead boy - I can't even remember his name, let's call him Skinhead - Skinhead asked, 'Was Hitler gay? Because there was this documentary on Channel 5 last night that said he was.'

Mr. Mudguard responded with the kind of detailed explanation that Skinhead wasn't really after.

'There are lots of theories that people offer to give a reason for why Hitler was a psychopath. One of these is whether or not it was his sexuality. I can't really understand that his sexuality would lead to him committing genocide. There are other just as fanciful reasons, for example, like he was raped by Jews, but the fact is that regarding his sexual preferences, his preference was to be pissed on by his niece.'

Skinhead was not satisfied with this explanation, so he decided to ask other boys in the class if they were gay. Loudly he asked his neighbour, an angry fat boy, in full earshot of an attentive class. 'NO!' came the emphatic reply. I wasn't really immediately taking in what he was saying, but the question had the act of Chinese Whispers about it. From boy to boy, 'Are you gay?' 'NO!' etc. etc. On and on it went, until it reached me.

'Yes, yes,' I said. 'Yes, yes,' instead of 'No, no!'

I remember saying it with such indifference. 'Yes'.

It was the boy in front of me, some floppy-haired guy, who was astounded that I had said yes. Floppy went, 'Seriously?' with disbelief, and I restated my affirmative, pretending to carry on with my work, as if nothing seismic had happened. 'No, you're not!' He demanded I retract the acknowledgement of my gayness, at which, newly liberated that it had actually happened, I said, 'Yes, I am!' Floppy's disbelief quickly turned into a horrified smirk. He nudged his neighbour and said, 'He just admitted he's gay,' to which the neighbour said, 'Whatever.' Floppy got him to ask me again, 'Are you gay?' and now, a bit bored by the whole thing, I said 'Yes!'

The same reaction came. Shock, denial, smirk and mock horror. It started to spread like wildfire, from one neighbour to the next, and the next, and the next! I tried to carry on with my work. I wasn't significantly bothered by the attention. It was new to me. I was usually just one of the boys that merged into the scenery. Mercifully, the bell went before the news reached Skinhead, the genesis of all the nonsense.

When I tell people this story, they usually react in two distinctively different and hyperbolic ways

1. 'Wow! That was so brave' or

2. 'What? That was so stupid'.

Really, it was neither. It was simply a boy being asked if he was gay, and him responding with 'yes'.

I had no idea what would happen next. I didn't really think about it. My mind was full of obsessive-compulsive rubbish about making sure the loops of my ls on my joined up handwriting matched, or whether before the end of the lesson the Earth might spin off its axis and scream towards the sun.

Following my outing in the History class, things slowly began to change. My lunch and break time tête-a-têtes with Ash, Blob and Gollum became a little fraught. They already knew I was gay, which hadn't really caused that much friction. They had, in fact, served as a go-between for an early crush of mine, a small albino boy whose name I've forgotten, when they had researched facts for me about him.

I guess the only thing to be said for indulging in a *Bastardography* is that you recalibrate memories and feelings you had soiled in self-hatred, and dial them back to the innocent fun and sweetness they once possessed. If only the same could be done with chewing gum. But I did have crushes, oh, did I have crushes!

A dark-eyed, pale-skinned, fit-as-fuck, 29 year old, semi-professional football-playing, suit-wearing, smile-suggesting, cheeky, jack-the-lad French teacher. A teacher I never 'had' in any sense of the word. No such luck. But in my thirteen year old state, Mr. Baker was every young boy's dream. Ever since the time I saw him flit in and out of a lesson to whisper something into the ear of our Head of Year – I knew, I just knew he was beauty personified. A perfect man. Educated, classically handsome, a sense of humour, fluent in French, played football to a competent standard and could certainly pull off his tracksuit bottoms – oh, how they'd cling!

For the next few weeks I'd spend most of my lunchtimes hovering outside the window that looked into his classroom as he marked work, drank protein shakes or surreptitiously scratched his balls. I knew he knew I was watching him. Occasionally he'd look up and I'd hide, only to return to my vantage point when I thought enough time had passed. I don't know how long this went on for, but it prompted some vivid dreams, and even some satirical fiction for my English coursework.

One day, after a brain-draining double Maths, I rushed to the window of my darling crush. But he wasn't there. I then heard a rather melodramatically affected cough. I turned, and there he was, all six foot three of him.

'I'm sure you can think of better things to do with your time than stare at me through the window!' he monotoned, with the same cold, uncaring flatness that every future queen would reject me with! But before I had a chance to reply, 'No, you're beautiful,' he was gone. He made a point of never, ever speaking to me again, and I made a point of never, ever looking at him again through that window. My crush had been crushed.

Now during the breaktime sojourns where we'd previously had a laugh and a joke, came unwelcome interruptions from complete strangers. 'Hey, are you the guy that admitted he's gay?' To which of course, I'd reply with, 'Yes', though after the twelve-dozenth boy came up to me and asked, it began to get a little boring. Sometimes they would just go, 'Oh okay,' and walk off. Sometimes they'd bring others to marvel at my response, and some would ask follow up questions. 'Do your parents know?' 'No', 'When did you know?' 'I think since I was eight,' and so on and so on. Some were quite innocent and curious. Others were foul and vile, and those were the people who just wanted to be cunts about it.

'Do you take it up the arse?' was a common question. The fact that I was a virgin and had no idea how to have sex other than what I'd seen in porn (an incredibly poor sex education by anyone's standards) made it a bit of a silly ask. The questions became a bit demoralising. I sometimes questioned them back as to why they were so interested, to which they'd say, 'I've never met anyone gay before,' which was also absurd.

It was fascinating how quickly the school became suddenly interested in me. A month before, no one really knew who I was other than my three freaky friends. Now, I was notorious. I couldn't walk down the corridor without someone shouting, 'Queer!' 'Faggot!' or something similarly unimaginative. It was never challenged by any teacher who observed it, which I found incomprehensible. I'd just walk on. I never really challenged it either, and the truth is, at that point, it still didn't really bother me.

What did begin to bother me was the violence. It was almost like a social experiment. How far does a group have to go to crush the resistance of the individual? Every lesson I was in soon offered at least one person who liked to cause trouble by making an example of me. In registration every morning and afternoon there was a boy who sat behind me, Freckles, who just chirped up one day with abuse, which I initially ignored.

He then threw stuff at me, striking me on the back of the head with a sharp lump of broken plastic. No reaction.

Another time it was a dousing of pencil sharpenings, all pretty tame stuff. Then, out of nowhere, he sprayed the back of my head with an aerosol and then struck a match, I jumped out of my skin and managed to get away in time, but I was astounded at his violence. He always prefaced some creative attack (tacks on the chair, FAG etched onto my desk, and so on) with some damning eulogy to my sexual orientation. I never seemed to fight back outright; I just took it all with a vague boredom. Also, I never thought that there were obviously other gay, bisexual, trans and alternative young men in my class who would've observed what was happening to me as a stark warning to not be true to themselves, or would have to learn from the revelation that being true to yourself comes at a price.

As this, shall we call it 'bullying' - it's a word, I guess, but a feebly umbrella term - developed, it became more a focal point for mine and Gina's regular conversations. She became a bit of a Mother Confessor for me. I was allowed to ditch lessons to go and talk to her. She became my refuge. I asked her whether any other boys met her like this.

Gina took a deep breath. 'There was another boy in the year above you. Last year.'

'What happened?' I asked, already imagining some perfect older boy with golden locks and eyes like sapphires.

'Well, he was being bullied, and he took an overdose in the RE class. He texted his best friend and told him what he was going to do, and Miss Trent found him. They had to call an ambulance and everything.'

I was rather shocked.

'He's back now, doing okay.'

I was even more shocked. I had so many questions, but she wouldn't go into too much detail. She was obviously not meant to talk about it. I wanted to know who it was so I could seek him out, and he could save me.

'Does he still get bullied?' I asked.

'No, they called a big assembly and the Head of Year had a go at all of them, saying that they, ultimately, were responsible for his overdose.' It was almost as if Gina was saying, 'Try to top yourself and they'll leave you alone,' but I didn't have that in me.

After I found out about the boy, I started to stalk most Year 11 classes, including after school clubs. I think I found him, although I was never sure. There was a cool alternative boy with long hair, wearing a Slipknot top under his school shirt, and with indie wristbands. All of that. I have no idea if it was him. He seemed gay to me, or at least someone confident enough to be different. I even followed him about half a mile one afternoon. Never spoke to him though. Shame.

The turning point where the bullying got out of hand finally came. It was around the time Jimmy Hall got involved. He wasn't in the same school house as me and I was only subjected to him in art. However, he took a sociopathic glee in humiliating me. During art, he'd sing songs about me, scrawl anti-gay graffiti over my books and be relentless in his efforts to make me an example. All that was in my armoury was a disapproving stare, to which he'd react angrily with, 'Don't You Fucking Dare Look At Me Like That, You Faggot!'

He said it with such anger. I couldn't stare him out. He was the type of boy that would never back down. So I let him go to town on me. He didn't even need to wait for the teacher to go out of the room, because Mr. Startled, a devout Christian, loved to hear James' homophobic waffle. He'd use anything as a starting point for a monologue about how gay I was. Mr. Startled found this most amusing. Hall would do stuff like grab one of the hooked poles that open the tall classroom windows, get some of his droog mates to hold my arms down while he simulated stuffing the end of the pole into my arse. He also tried to do something similar with the end of a compass, I can't recall quite what. There was a lot of this cruel and unusual punishment dotted about during those months. This was around autumn 2002, a time when it started to pick up and become really dangerous.

A typical day might start by being accosted in the library to hear how I loved sucking my dad's cock. I would then spend double Maths trying to un-deface and salvage my exercise book. I would run from lesson to lesson to avoid being spotted and subjected to a mauling. Boys didn't want to sit next to me anymore, so I'd sit at the back, on my own.

The end of school was the most dangerous time of the day. One particularly unpleasant event occurred when I was chatting with Ash, and I did the silly leg gallop thing Basil Fawlty does, which some boy saw and accused me of being a faggot for doing it. He didn't really need an excuse. He decided to pull me about, push me over and kick me hard in the stomach. I tried to walk on with Ash when he stopped, but he hadn't finished. More kicks came. I just went as limp as possible and let him do it.

When he'd finished, Ash had gone, so I walked on alone to the bus stop. I was in a post-beating daze when I felt something sharp hit my cold ear. Then another sharp hit struck the back of my head. I turned and saw three younger boys. They must have been in year seven or eight and they began pelting with me with stones and small rocks. I could hear one go, 'It's the gay one'. I picked up speed and ran on, luckily reaching the bus stop as the bus arrived, and got on it. They hit the window of the bus with more rocks as it drove on.

My diaries at the time (I eventually destroyed them) detailed, in a line, experiences like: 'I had stones thrown at me by younger boys,' but I never really described how it all made me feel. I didn't ever link my depression to it. But I did have bouts of completely disassociated depression, where I was so ill I felt no connection to reality at all. I would think real life wasn't really real. The whole death / existence / fear stuff was now my life 24/7. I just wasn't really there.

Around this time my sister started seeing a man whom I disliked greatly. So much so, I came to call him 'pig in a vest'. The family also greatly loathed him, all of them except my sister. She moved in with him in a little place in SW19, along with their dog. We'd visit occasionally but it was always a bit awkward as Pig was often moody and my sister and I still argued a lot then. I never thought the relationship would amount to much, because my sister's last boyfriend, who had red hair, now seemed in hindsight a lot better. But she had got rid of him, and I thought Pig would go much the same way. It came as an absolute shock when my mum announced to me and my dad that my sister was pregnant! In a melodramatic way, I dropped a full cup of tea, on purpose, to illustrate my shock.

This has all perhaps been painted as a world of doom and gloom, and, yes, a lot of it was indeed grey and miserable. But even in the most desolate wasteland, pretty things can grow… I was still making films. Now I was spending most of the time on my own, I would make stop-motion animations.

In my own passive way I had managed to expel some of the ill feeling that was building around me, and to stand up subtly. In RE we had to describe suffering in a poem or a picture. I chose the former and wrote something rather basic, but I owe it to my fourteen year old self to copy it out here to document those times:

'I have to suffer it every single school day,'
I think when I'm walking to school,
I bet they analyse the way I speak,
Everyone stares as I walk through the door,
They probably think I'm such a freak,
Hearing the same questions is such a bore,
You'd think they'd never seen anyone gay before,
I don't really mind the questions, they're just immature.

I have to suffer it every single school day,
I can't even escape during morning break,
They come up, with all sorts of things to ask,
They don't understand, they think I'm a fake,
They ask stupid questions, 'Do your parents mind?'
They wait silently for some sort of answer,
'I haven't told them, I'll think you'll find.'

I have to suffer it every single school day,
It's constant, there's always someone looking for me,
So at lunch I find some kind of hideaway,
And you're always grateful when you find someplace,

But somehow they always manage to find me,
It's all too much, they're always in my face.

I have to suffer it every single school day,
Even when it's time to go home,
And as if from nowhere they appear,
When I am waiting at the bus stop,
I want to run away, collapse and cry,
They ask more questions and I have to reply.

Seamus Heaney, eat your heart out.

It's interesting to note that even though Section 28 hadn't been repealed at this point, this piece of work was displayed on the wall of the RE classroom, where it had homophobic abuse scrawled all over it by students. But I liked the fact that my RE teacher had displayed it publicly. It was a little moment of solidarity.

Other solidarity was less welcome, especially the manic, super-stressed Mr. Horne, a husky-voiced, bulging-eyed walking vein. And a vein that looked like it was about to burst at any moment. He was our PSHE teacher and very forward-thinking. He taught us about masturbation and did touch on gay sex and relationships a bit in class, though that just made Freckles taunt me with, 'Did you hear? Horne said it's okay to be gay now,' before jabbing a biro into my arm.

Horne was a libertarian, a man constantly on edge. He pissed me off no end when Gina and I began a rather grown-up fight-back to the bullying problem. We explained about me being out and then about the backlash, and Mr. Horne's response was, 'So what? That's not your problem. You carry on as you are. It's their behaviour that's out of order here!' I knew what he meant. He wanted to treat it like it was no big deal me being gay and that we should just get on with it. Unfortunately at the time this wasn't something that worked. I was so pissed off at his supposed solution to my problem that one day when I waited outside Gina's room (which was next to his) and a boy didn't quite make the toilet and vomited a thick endless orange porridge down the WC's doorjamb. Horne ran out and shouted at him, 'What are you doing?' I jumped in with, 'You should be helping him, not shouting at him'. My comment stopped him in his tracks, and he barked, 'I see your point'. Then in his frenetic way, he started to scoop up all the sick with the edge of his files.

Subjecting Horne to such indignities did little to assuage the horror of the daily twattery from my fellow classmates. It was clearly getting to me, whether I realised it or not. It got to the point where I began to feign illness to try to get off school, but my mum knew the dodge and would often force me to go in anyway. She feels guilty about this now as she had no real idea of what was going on then, and I can't blame her. In the end I started to play truant. It wasn't a conscious act. My legs would turn to lead as I trudged over the bypass towards the school. I'd walk more and more slowly until I came to a virtual standstill. I'd sit under a tree in the field nearby until enough time had passed and then I would get the bus into Sutton where I would end up hiding in the library until it was time for school to end, and then I'd go over to my Nan's.

I managed to get away with this about three or four times, until one day when I decided to go to Woolworths for some pick 'n' mix before my daily library trip. A harsh-sounding woman called over to me, 'Excuse me! Can you come here please?' Such a battle-axe. I ignored her and carried on shovelling fuzzy milk-bottles into my cup. I then felt a big hand grab my shoulder.

'Young man, listen to the woman!' I turned round and towering over me was a policeman, complete with titted helmet. He had the tone of cockney bobby. It was all so clichéd. 'Shouldn't you be in school?' he asked with the tone of You've Done Something Terribly Wrong. I was mute. Everyone in the shop was looking at me. Young mothers with prams were tutting, and old couples shook their heads. I couldn't say anything. I just nodded. I was paraded out through the shop and into a waiting panda car.

I was silent throughout the policeman's law rap. 'You shouldn't play truant as you can get into a lot of trouble, and you're at risk. A young boy like you, out on his own. No-one knows where you are… You're much safer at school.'

It was at that moment that I broke down in tears. The idea that I was being taken back to a place where they broke bottles over my head and smashed my face into the brick wall was safer? This was the clearest indication that there was no order to the universe and that no one had a fucking clue!

Mr. Mudguard was there to greet me when I arrived. He knew why I was truanting and he let me sit at the back of a sixth form class for the rest of the afternoon. I was let off games and other concessions were made. But school went on, to the point where I had no fight left in me. Even my few remaining friends had cut me out. 'Oh that was a great night out on Friday when…' they bragged about their adventures in front of me, detailing how they'd gone out together without me. 'We would invite you, but our parents don't want you

there. It's not because you're gay, they just think you're insane.'
Oh that's alright, then.

In the end I just refused to go in. I told them unequivocally that I would never step foot inside the school again. My mother agreed. Shortly before this, I had told my parents by letter the whole story of my coming out, and about the abuse I had suffered. I left it on the table in the morning and went to school. When I came back in the evening I found it had been opened and read.

My dad, who had hitherto been homophobic and vocal on the subject for many years, suddenly seemed very quiet. Not supportive, but not nasty. My mum rang up the school and told them I wouldn't be going back. Meetings were set up with my parents, Gina and my Head of Year to discuss what might happen now, and they decided that they should try and get me into the Hospital and Individual Tuition Service. This was, as they put it, intimate schooling for adolescents who were not in mainstream education because they had mental health problems, or simply couldn't cope with the mainstream environment.

In all that time, through all that bullying, friends treating me like shit, violence, name-calling, and general cruelty, the only thing that stands out in my memory so much that it still has the power to hurt me is this:

I was waiting for the bus one particular afternoon after school, and the Scouse boy with the fluorescent yellow teeth turned up and sat near me. We'd been on chatting terms, and I hadn't seen him for a while, certainly not since I'd come out. I struck up a friendly conversation as we always did, yet this time he didn't respond. He looked at me, with this look of, not fear or hatred, not of anything. He just looked at me and turned away. We sat there beside one another, in silence. That look will stay with me forever.

It felt like this was the moment when, because of the pariah status I had been rendered, this person now didn't even have to recognise me as anything. Some would argue I couldn't really know what he was thinking. Maybe he wanted to reach out but couldn't, or maybe he was having some similar problem, or maybe it was something entirely unrelated to me. The thing was, I took it as that, and I let it happen. I didn't question it. I just accepted that now this was how someone could treat me.

5.
DRAPERS

'No one is so brave that he is not disturbed by something unexpected.'

Julius Caesar

The whole process of getting me into the Hospital and Individual Tuition Service (also known historically as the Drapers School) took nearly three months. I was fifteen by this point, and halfway through my GCSE coursework assignments. I lived quite near my now 'old school' and some of the boys who bullied me still lived in roads adjacent to mine. There were only one or two incidents where I was shouted at by them, or chased on bikes, but in my head I began to build up a morbid fear of going outdoors because even the thought of them looking at me was unbearable.

I snuck out once a week to see Gina, who also had an office outside of the school, and we ended up talking again, mostly about things I was interested in: my writing, the things I would watch on telly, that sort of thing. She really was the only person I had to talk honestly to.

She drove me in her car to this new 'tuition service' where I was soon introduced to all the teachers. It seemed such a small and friendly place. My demeanour by then had changed considerably. I was now completely quiet and entirely detached. I lived in a private fantasy (or nightmare) in my head, and the things that were going on around me simply passed me by without my noticing.

Drapers was then like a little hutch, green and prefab, just plonked down behind old hospital grounds. It was set so far back in the grounds of the old hospital that it took a good fifteen minute walk from the main street just to reach it. Well secluded, we shared the grounds with a home for severely disabled people. The cries of the brain-damaged, the autistic and the undiagnosed rang out unheeded as we drove up the yellow brick road.

The teeniest of little buildings overlooked a farm, acres of land and of all things equine. I was shown around and shook lots of hands. In this instance, I remarked, 'I feel like Princess Margaret,' but in all honesty, even in my darkest hour, I've neither felt nor looked that rough.

I met Kate, the headmistress, who had this strange look as if she'd been hit over the head with a blunt instrument. She possessed one of those dead stares, not unaffected by rivulet scars around her mouth; of course these may just have been crevices. She was also the drama teacher, so I softened to her immediately. There was Mrs. Silver in her little bobble hat (Science), Mrs. Crowther with her hairy forearms (Maths) - I think this was the result of either the menopause or diabetes - I forget which. There was Mrs. Fenn, with one of those permanently hoarse voices, scrawny bodies and a propensity for lycra; one I could tell was going to be highly strung (Art).

I found it refreshing that most of the teachers were female. There was Belinda, who taught PSHE, who was an immediate delight. I knew I liked her because my desire and commensurate potential to show off heightened in her presence. This also happened when I met Ed, who looked a bit like a thin Richard Nixon mixed with Max Wall, although only for a brief moment, because during our introduction he got a phone call and had to run off somewhere.

The tour lasted all of five minutes, as the size of my new school was about as big as the inside of a small flat. I liked the look of it. What was even more exciting was that there were boys there. Boys, although the few sexually ambiguous ones clearly hated the very skin they inhabited.

For my first few days there I was driven to school by my parents, with my dad making the hilarious gag on the first day as we drove past Carslake Boys, 'Shall I make a left'?'

We got to wear our own clothes. This was another worry, because I hadn't a stitch to wear. Not literally: I had clothes, but by this time, my penchant for fashion was somewhat lacking. I went in for a completely shaven head, cheap t-shirts and jeans, even cheaper trainers (you can often tell if someone's exhibiting a high level of mental distress if they wear *Shoe Zone* trainers). To top it all off I had this beige Puffa jacket, which I would always put the hood up on whenever I trudged around. What a sight! I am sure my mum pleaded with me to get new clothes, but it was too late by now to worry about 'making an impression'.

After a week or two of being driven there, I settled in, and my parents thought it'd be better if I got the bus. I was bricking it, but they both had work and there was no other way around the situation. My aversion to being seen by anyone from school became so great that I would run from my front door to the bus stop as fast as I could every morning, hood up, no matter what the weather. I'd sit at the front of the bus, single seat if I could, head turned, earphones in. I was terrified. The fear was so great that seeing anyone my age would cause me to freak out. It wouldn't matter even if they weren't someone who had bullied me, just so long as they were associated with those who had. They didn't have to be unpleasant, just their existence would make me feel physically ill. This is where my mass avoidance kicked in.

I still behaved completely irrationally the few times someone from the old school took time out of their day to actually say hello to me. One time it was the boy from a few doors down who had the audacity to ask me for a cigarette. He was the one who had once laughed at me as I was being attacked. I replied, without looking at him, 'No, fuck off,' with a flat indifference. I can still see his blinking disbelief at my words. He even repeated them back to me quizically, '*Fuck off?*' Strange I'd still speak out, a year after the fact.

Whenever it was groups of boys, though, I stayed clear. They were generally on bikes and would shout abuse, and it could get nasty. Looking back on it, I had utter shits as 'friends', because after all I had been through, it still took about four months for anyone to actually ring me. In the end it was Gollum, who with a stifled laugh asked me, 'Why haven't you been at school for months?' I made up some impossible lie that I'd broken my arm and I'd be returning when it was healed. His response was a knowing, 'Oh we thought you'd left because of all the bullying'. I denied the rumour and said I'd be seeing them soon.

Nothing after that.

Nothing.

That was all I got for three and a half years of friendship. Now I understand why Quentin Crisp said worthwhile relationships need you to give and give and give.

Still I didn't need to worry about the old crap friends.

I had new crap friends to make. Oh dear, I don't want this to sound bitter. It's meant to be irreverent and humorous. I hardly think of these moments now. It's just for the purposes of the book - *honest!*

Yes, I got on okay with everyone at Drapers. There was Arnold with his little button nose and half-broken voice who was obsessed with rappers, even though he was a scrawny little white boy. I feigned an interest. He even gave me a ripped CD of Kanye West and Obie Trice, although Obie did have a few nice ditties. Then there was Jacob who was a lanky mixed-race celery stick with a few anger issues.

You could never really tell what anyone was in there for. The facts never emerged. It was perfect. I wasn't out to anyone at Drapers, although I am sure the staff knew, because, I imagine, there must have been files on us. There was a girl called Lana that I was chummy with at first. A cockney girl with blonde hair and the intelligence of a tit mouse. No, strike that. A brain-damaged tit mouse. She was the one that got me into smoking because she and some of the other kids congregated outside, and I felt left out. Oh, peer pressure!

I was terrified of having male friends. I needn't have worried. The only boys I liked had no interest in me. Shaun was one such boy. He had skin like porcelain, jet black hair, great cheekbones. He was a gorgeous skater-boi type. Apparently he had some terrible insomnia problem. We sometimes walked down to the bus stop, but we were hardly close. He was friendly with Matthew, a boy who had a casually spiteful homophobic streak in him. He was really odd. He'd say things like, 'Oh I love Red Dwarf. My favourite character is Lister'. I'd say, 'Mine's Rimmer,' and he would say, 'Of course, he's such a faggot'. That was odd, as Rimmer, despite his name, was not a gay character.

Matthew was a self-harmer. That interested me. I had also heard from someone that his father died when he drove his jeep off the edge of a cliff or something, so I kind of forgave his homophobia. People occasionally would ask about my sexuality which I never confirmed or denied, unless I had to. I wouldn't say yes as I was too terrified of the reaction. I do regret not coming out to Keith, though, because even though he was a troublemaker, he really needed a gay ally, to help him come to terms with himself. I just couldn't be there for him at that moment.

There's not much point talking about the lessons, though. The truth is I never did much during my time there. I just zoned out. I couldn't care less. I had no interest in my future. I loathed my past. But I did enjoy my present. I really had a good time at Drapers. People were nice. There was the odd element of a threat. Only occasionally did one of the kids from the Youth Offending Team in the next block burst into one of our lessons threatening to cut off their electronic tag and wrap it round our throats.

The first proper friend I made at Drapers was a girl, Francesca, who was totally crazy. She was friendly, and there was a bit of a spark there. Her mother was murdered and I think this had left her with a lot of problems (no shit, Sherlock). We got close. We sat and smoked in the park by the Sainsbury's in East Cheam. I had dinner at hers. When the wind howled she said it was the ghost of her mother. She'd often lapse into telling me details of the grizzly case that had changed her life. I just nodded. Her dad was also friendly, even though he loved the music of Shania Twain. Francesca frightened me, though. She was totally unhinged. She'd be prone to sudden flights of rage, where she would describe how she'd once got into a fight and bottled a girl in the street, 'Breaking a bottle and then grinding it round and around her gums'.

Then a goth walked into my life and it was all okay for a bit. It was interesting when the goth showed up, because none of the other girls liked her. They were freaked out by her, as were the boys. I loved that. She waltzed in that first time, with her ten-inch high electric-punk stiletto heels, all in black. Piercings all over her face, tattoos all over her arms, make-up round her eyes, blonde hair styled à la ridiculously outlandish. She was an outcast angel. I did my 'Would you like a cigarette?' routine or I lit hers or something. She seemed stand-offish at first, but she was the sweetest little pixie ever. If a little racist.

As my first proper term at Drapers drew to a close, I'd established a system. I'd go in for morning class if I could be bothered, but definitely would be in for the afternoon class. Yes - we had just two lessons a day. I'd scrape along with the bare minimum, making jokes and wise-cracks throughout, especially if it was English. Then it would be the death-defying trip back on the bus, avoiding being spotted. My evening would be spent watching an unhealthy amount of *Friends* episodes which I remember laughing so hard at, that I would weep.

The 'once every four month' catch up sessions with 'Twitch' came to an end. They were so far apart that she wasn't even aware I had been bullied or why, except that she felt we didn't need the sessions any more, seeing as my parents had cajoled me into saying it wasn't helpful.

The thing that was going to happen that scared me more than anything wasn't going to this new place. It was the fact that Gina would be leaving the counselling service and going back to Australia. We had a number of sessions left, and we even had lunch together the last time. She said she would be back at the counselling service twice more to do some Saturday clinic thing, but it felt as though it was over.

The new routine was very simple. We had a three day week, and only two, two hour lessons. The rest of the time was spent at home smoking, cutting[25] or writing my diary. I was fine around the other pupils. All were as self-absorbed as I was, although their problems were more apparent than mine. The pyromaniac, the one who had Asperger's, the narcoleptic, and so on. I was just inert and quiet. The only thing I vaguely offered up as a persona was my dour, miserable and self-deprecating disposition. The humour was mixed in later when I felt more safe, but I made no reference whatsoever to my sexuality, and on the occasion I was asked, I evaded it by saying, 'none of your business', or 'why do you want to know?' or most ashamedly 'no'. It had become a problem.

After Gina, the only person who I had any support from was one of the teachers, who I got on quite well with, Ed (yes, we used teachers' first names and got to wear our own clothes). Unfortunately he was always very busy and I only saw him a few times to chat with, and those times I wasted by telling him wild fantasies about some boy I loved and had met, when no such encounters had taken place. Even with him I had to do the whole 'mention lots of writers that are gay but are not overt' bit, and try and get the conversation to go that way. I still had not yet been able to say it outright.

---

25 just slipped that one in, didn't I - self-harm, now, is it? Well I've minimised the inclusion, so as not to trigger anyone who is still suffering, to keep the blade-addiction at bay, but I'm sure I'll go on again about it later.

* * *

Towards the end of my last year at school, at the time when we sat our examinations, I was at a very low ebb. I failed all of my exams, purposefully not trying, and making absolutely no effort to make plans to go to college. The only positive step I made was to get an appointment with my G.P.. Luckily I didn't get the family doctor, but a sympathetic young woman, who I more or less pleaded with to get me referred again back to the Mental Health Team, which she did.

This next move, like any that looks to avail itself of the NHS Mental Health Services, took a long time coming. By now my life had become one entirely spent sitting around the house, and planning out my day to the rhythm of the television schedule, becoming slowly more and more isolated and deluded.

When the NHS finally cranked itself into gear, the first psychiatrist I saw was a pleasant middle-aged man called Dr. Sayed, refined and intelligent, chatty and humorous. The sessions were comfortable, and although I'd tested the waters in my usual way about the sexuality lark, I still couldn't actually bring myself to say the G word. It again passed under the radar.

After the assessment, he made the conclusion that I should have one-on-one psychotherapy. The idea of getting to talk about myself with someone's undivided attention three times a week seemed most gratifying. Also there was a young woman therapist present which also helped, but still there was a resistance. I would talk about everything to do with the bullying, except why, although of course there were so many other things to talk about, more pressing matters.

It didn't rear its head quite as often as you'd think. But then the not being able to tell her whenever it was brought up, felt like a problem. I had severe paranoid feelings that she'd be disgusted, shout at me and tell me to leave, and I'd end up the suicide victim of a mad psychotherapist in some pathetic tabloid story. Fanciful stuff, but then, remember, I was mad at the time.

I continued to regularly see Dr. Cohn, my psychotherapist. It was the only time I got out of the house each week, but shortly after my seventeenth birthday, I became severely depressed. I didn't sleep for seven days, and became more and more confused until I finally broke down completely.

These fragmented entries were among the last things I wrote before I had myself voluntarily committed as an inpatient at Springfield University Psychiatric Hospital between January and June 2005.

Had an odd dream last night. I was in KFC, and Gollum was waving from the bus stop on the opposite side of the road. I knocked past him and ran across the car park towards a grassy ditch covered by a section of a fallen tree branch. Curious, I lifted it, and underneath there was a dead baby, grey, twisted and lifeless. Naked except for a nappy. The side of its hairless head had been battered in and was bruised, rotten even, like an old neglected apple. Its left eye had been poked out and was teeming with luminous yellow maggots. I scooped these out with the edge of a white piece of paper that suddenly appeared in my hand. The baby's mother was beside me, weeping. I wanted to turn to her and say, 'It's only a doll', but could not bring myself to do it.

* * *

Oh, next year I must 'do' something to stop myself going mad, and start to really live. I suppose I'll ask Dr. Cohn about it on January 4th. I could start taking walks early each morning around the block in no particular direction at all, always knowing (at the back of my mind) that I will wind up back at my house, my home, my place.

* * *

DAY ONE OF GETTING BETTER

Such anticipation, such a longing to put down in actual words, into sentences. I don't even believe I can put it all down in words in one go.

To put it simply, truthfully.

I am going to write down all the pain I have inside my head, candidly and unashamedly, from now on, in this diary.

I am impatient to get it all out, as I should after over a year of hating myself privately, and hating others openly, showing my utter contempt for them, and holding a (wrongful) belief that I am the one to blame for all my unhappiness, my depression, my self-loathing.

I am opening up to myself in full plain uncritical detail, my life and the reasons I am depressed.

The foundation is that I Am Not To Blame, That Society Is Not To Blame, That My Family Are Not To Blame. Now, they are to 'blame' for the past, purposeful commas because blame is a mini-sweeping statement of a word, but I will eventually delve into that with Dr. Cohn.

I have also held my diaries to ransom, demanding from them something they cannot possibly offer: A Solution To All My Problems! This cannot work if I am scurrying away and writing down how I Feel About Myself, Hating Myself, From The Smallest Detail To The Largest Parts Of Myself!

There remains an intense suppressed fear which has rotted through my mind, and has nearly destroyed me, eating its way through me like some mental cancer. I have hidden from myself the real me for so long, that the only thing to help me, was to privately purge myself of intense self-loathing. All of me. Every little bit. To scurry away.

Now Mr. Hetherington started to untangle my mind, as did Gina before she went back to Australia. Mr. Hetherington was never around, but I told both of them as much as I wanted to, not all, because I am terrified of anything I don't know or understand. Also I have a shame, an intense sickening numbing fear, (you must understand, that I am now writing in a way as if I am talking to someone who will help me), because I have had it drummed into me that 'you do not count, nothing about you counts, nothing you do counts, you are nothing!' That is what I have been taught by my father, my grandparents and my sister, not directly, but through the feeling of manipulation and mistrust which comes from the fact that they say they still love me.

Now I am getting to the meat of the story. I don't want to yet, though. I will talk to Dr. Cohn about it, then write my opinions about her suggestions and I will take it on board. A lot of it comes from the bullying. I am upset even to recall a lot of it. This whole willingness to try, a real willingness to try, a willingness to talk about it to Dr. Cohn, firstly about avoiding to tell her I'm gay. I know that it will be immensely difficult to maintain the belief that I will become a well-balanced individual, mature for my age, proud of my age. As for my sexuality - that's the big one!

Firstly, it is to accept (not admit, admit is a bad word) my intelligence. I know I will look back on this and have a 'tender contempt' for myself, and that my motives are very different in the here and now. I've got to believe in myself. I've got to no longer suppress the way I feel and to pick at the massive knotted web of my mind. And I've got to trust myself and my own abilities. To trust what I like. I have accepted all my problems and will feel depressed from time to time, a 'deep despair'. I can call in my journal type entries, but I am going to trust my mind, myself. I feel incredibly vulnerable and weak (physically) at first, but I am now shuffling less. I Accept All Of My Problems and am willing to face them, untangle them and do practical things.

I know there will be lapses, but I am determined to look deep inside myself with confidence, to stop feeling like a nervous little five year old. To not make sweeping criticisms about everything all the time, like my alcoholic Uncle Steven. I need positive male role-models to become a positive man, intelligent ones. It is bewildering, but depression is an illness. I trust that fact, I am going to take it one tiny step at a time. I am under no illusion that it's going to be a long, drawn out and painstakingly slow process.

* * *

With a hand under each arm I was taken from the pink-fendered Renault 5, my purple trainers dragging along the concrete path, through to the local Child and Adolescent Mental Health Services. In my sleep-deprived state the only thought that didn't involve ghosts, conspiracies to poison my food or spontaneous human combustion, was the desire to smoke. But sparking up wasn't considered on in hospital premises, even in 2005. So I was promptly relieved of my stash by my mum.

My parents had been looking after me round the clock since I had stopped sleeping. They've been looking after me most of the time since I was born, and still do to this day. But I was then in particularly desperate need of assistance.

I was a rambling, terrified and confused wreck. I couldn't make sense of anything around me. My psychiatrist first prescribed an anti-psychotic sedative, which knocked me out for one night, but as soon as I woke I was exactly the same as I had been before.

I met twice with Dr. Cohn, my parents having to drive me there with me shouting the whole way that we were going to crash. I wasn't making any sense, and Dr. Sayed passed my notes sealed in an envelope to my mum and told my parents to take me to St. George's, where I saw the head of the entire region, or something. I was a little preoccupied at the time. She was a psychiatrist, you can be sure of that. Apparently, I was later told this. I have no recollection, but I was asking to be put into hospital because I didn't feel safe. This woman who I saw agreed, and told me that I could volunteer myself as an inpatient in an adolescent ward at Springfield, Tooting, called Aquarius.

I agreed.

6.

AGE OF AQUARIUS

Another Haiku

Boy's happy at last!
Friends, pills, bed. Free to look out
Wooden bar windows.

'We do not have to visit a madhouse to find disordered minds; our planet is the mental institution of the universe.'

Johann Wolfgang von Goethe

'Can you sign your name here, here, and again, here?' a nurse asked.

I could barely see, but the form had duplicates so I knew it was kosher, and signed away. It was a list of the clothes I was wearing. 'Can you just pop on the scales?' the nurse asked again, her flutey monotonous voice caught in the endless repetition of her daily instructions. I was aware of my parents being somewhere nearby, having a sit down. I thought it would be best when they weighed me to show them all the scars on my arms and legs. They weren't that interested, as it turned out.

After I was bagged and tagged by the staff, I was 'in'. It was then time for my parents to leave, which upset me greatly.

At seventeen I was still a homesick mummy's boy, and my mum looked broken to see me left there, out of my mind. My father told me later that afterwards my mum had cried all night at home, an image that haunts me still. I didn't move from the spot where they left for hours. I'd become obsessed by a leaflet stuck to the wall about menstruation, which had a diagram of a woman's innards.

One of the many delusions I'd succumbed to in my sleep-deprived state was that I had fallopian tubes and ovaries, something that my family had known and that I was never told about. One of the staff (apparently they were staff, though I couldn't really tell who was who - it seemed that if you were obese and had a big ring of keys hanging from your belt, then you were) encouraged me to sit for dinner. I didn't want to move from the leaflet, I planned to study it more closely.

One of the consequences of my anxiety was that I could not sit still and had to get up and move around as much as possible, not in any particular direction, just to pace and pace, a trait of the truly ill of mind. The pacing creates agitation but you feel that by walking you will somehow alleviate the feelings. All it does however is propel it further. I did manage to get to the dinner table, eventually. It was towards the back of the main common area. I was sort of getting my bearings by now. What really surprised me was that all the other patients were younger than me. Much younger than me. I was astounded. They looked like small children. The ward was for adolescents and 'young adults' so they couldn't be children. A part of me knew this but my vision was tricking me, presenting them as toddlers in fancy costumes.

I couldn't eat. The canteen served some odd slop, but I didn't want anything. There were several adults, dotted around the place, watching us, which didn't do much for the paranoid schizophrenics at the table. I noticed one person had their eyes on me. When I got up to pace again they'd follow. I'd become agitated and one thought I had was to maybe have a cigarette. To go for a smoke, you were taken through the area where we slept (one to a room) down a flight of stairs, out the fire exit and out into the courtyard. Here I could sit and smoke for as long as I liked, my knees bobbing up and down as I sucked on the filter in a few long scary drags.

When I got back to the ward the kids were playing *Mario Kart*, which was too bright and colourful a computer game for me. Every so often I was given a little yellow chalky pill, the reason for which I demanded to know. It was the Olanzapine that I had been prescribed a day or two ago, an anti-psychotic that was also used as a sedative. I kept saying I wasn't psychotic, which the staff agreed with, and said that anti-psychotics were used as part of a 'drug family' (I'm sure they're neighbours of ours) to deal with a number of mental health issues, including anxiety. I kept asking this, and in the end they printed off an information sheet I could keep with me to refer to.

The anxiety didn't abate that first night. As the hours wore in (rather than on), time started to not really make sense. My routine was: sit down, try to act calm and distract myself, get anxious, pace about, ask to go for a cigarette, go for cigarette, come back, sit down trying to act calm and distract myself, and so on. I carried on in this loop for what seemed like forever.

A shift in this pattern finally occurred when a young man with a camp Northern Irish accent took over. He had freckles and neatly styled short red hair. He was skinny and tall with green eyes and a few lone piercings. He told me that it would soon be time for bed, and that there was time for one more cigarette.

I don't know how I got into such a state in the courtyard. I can't recall my state of mind much, or even what time it was. I felt so overwhelmed, shaking on that little bench as the Belfast beauty watched me with his long translucent eyelashes fluttering. I didn't even realise I was doing it until I'd done it. I couldn't even feel below the waist. But wet patches don't lie. I'd pissed myself. Well it wasn't just a wet patch, it was a torrent of piss all down my jeans, splashing all over my trainers. I was taken to the showers to wash myself, but I couldn't understand how to turn the faucet on. I was given some shower gel to wash with, and I lathered it on myself, standing there trembling. I distinctly remember that the male nurse had to turn the shower on for me and sort of scrub off some of the excess gel. I wasn't in my right mind enough to enjoy it, alas.

And so to bed. For that it was, *sojourn*, complete with regulation 'spare jogging bottoms' and a nurse sitting by my bed through the night. They're supposed to sit outside the room when you're on 'suicide watch' but I had called out too much. I was just rabbiting on and on about a lot of nothing, which I worried about the next day, because I could've said something really crazy, like the truth! I was given lots of stuff through the night. I thought they were dosing me up good and proper. Turned out it was just Gaviscon for acid reflux.

The next morning, bizarrely, I felt a microscopic bit better, dazed and zombified and wandering, but not in as anxious a way this time. I didn't really say hello to anyone, although I was aware of people milling about, all now beginning to look a little more like young adults, I sat in the 'relaxation room', which was just a room with a bean bag in it and a bookshelf. The books must've been donated by a sadist, because I spent the morning flicking though a biography of Denis Healey. What horror![26]

I was the new boy. There seemed to be one appearing every day in the place.

The first people I got to know well were Janie and Zera who I went for ciggies with at the same time. They seemed personable and reassuringly ordinary. Zera always looked tired. She was a tiny little blonde sparrow of a thing with an arm almost beyond mutation from self-harm. It looked like something from an H. R. Giger painting. Janie looked like a grunger and spoke with a querulous tone as if she were always on the verge of crying, but she never did, strangely enough. These were at least two people you could have a conversation with, for what it was worth.

The boys didn't really have that much about them. Marlon, a dishy black boy, wandered about the place carrying an A4 sheet of paper with a print of a car on it. He never really spoke much. All I remember him doing was having occasional outbursts of anger and on one occasion he did this near my room and I had to hear him scream as they jabbed a needle full of sedative into him, before taking him to the 'cool-off room'. I think that was a euphemism for the old padded cell.

Our consultant psychiatrist looked like the Cowardly Lion so I couldn't really take him seriously. Also, he always had golf clubs in his office, which I've always found a big turn off. Most of the initial conversations were about the fact that

---

[26] I have nothing against Lord Healey per se (peace be upon him). Those eyebrows are enough to get anyone's motor running.

I was convinced I had some physical illness eating away at me like a brain tumour, or some rare condition that had been overlooked and would slowly kill me. A lot of blood samples were taken to abate these fears. You got a problem? Take a blood sample.

The next day was mum and dad's first visit. They seemed to like the place as I showed them round. 'Oooh, it's like student digs, isn't it, or a holiday camp.' They were both quite muted other than that and looked like they hadn't slept much.

As the boy who gets on with the teachers rather than the pupils, I got quite close to some of the staff and especially the Occupational Therapist, Clare. She looked like a character straight out of a Jacqueline Wilson novel with her spiky short hair, kooky jewellery and mad jumpers. Posh, but normal with it. It was with her that I got to have lots of informal chats about authors I liked, and she'd take me out so I could buy, cook and eat my own lunch.

One of the humiliations of being on an adolescent ward was the fact that there was a 'classroom' where we would do 'lessons'. Note my liberal use of air commas, as it was all a bit of a mock-up. It was to encourage routine. We'd go and sit in this air-conditioned room full of computers and safety scissors (only allowed to use them with careful supervision) and we'd be talked at by a woman with odd hair and a man who looked and acted like one of those blokes off Saturday Kitchen. You know the ones I mean, with the smiley face and trendy jeans even though they are middle-aged and a bit weird. Those were the 'teachers'.

We had this project we were supposed to work on, and this OBE visited us who had a long beard and did murals (not IRA ones) and talked to us like we were without brain capacity. He was very full of himself, more so than his creepily thin body would suggest. I can't recall actually doing any of the project activities. There was a trip to Tate Modern in the minibus where, due to an organisational oversight, there was an audio instillation of chattering voices in the turbine hall, not a good idea for the psychotics in the group. Also, our tour guide had worksheets and interactive felt samples that were written for toddlers.

It was a restful time, though. Once I got my bearings and finally slept a full night, I started to once again take control. I asked for the suicide watch to be called off. I wasn't really at any risk. I'm a suicidalist for the most part, I love the idea of extinguishing my life in a romantic go-to exit strategy, but I have never really made an attempt. I've got close. I've experimented, but if I were to go through with doing myself in, I'd just do it. No faffing.

I also stopped taking the anti-psychotics. I had to ask to be taken off them, because if they were on your pill chart (a nice little whiteboard with the roll call of our names) you had to take them. I was never much trouble to the screws - I mean mental health care assistants, or fake nurses. Consequently I wasn't given as much attention as Janie, who would use any opportunity to escape, whether she went via the fire escape (once the fire doors were open, the magnetic locks on all the doors in the ward would unfasten, and the lunatics could get out) and she'd try and throw herself in front of cars or run down to Tooting Bec Station to go under the tube. She was wrestled to the floor on the platform that time and brought back by her favourite carer who looked a lot like Coleen Nolan. Janie shook and wept, repeating the words, 'I really thought I was going that time.'

When not running, she and Zera (they were close, almost symbiotic) would take vast quantities of paracetamol and fall asleep a lot. This was an early sign of an overdose, which I didn't know before. If anyone on the ward seemed a bit dozy or sleepy they'd be taken for a blood test. I got tested often, not because I ever took an overdose but because I was often sleepy and dozy, a family trait, unfortunately. I got quite chummy with Janie, and I managed to come out to her in a very awkward way involving hangman clues (the inappropriate games we played to pass the time in the common area).

I really enjoyed spending time with her family who would often give me lifts, and I amused Janie's younger sister by making faces and telling jokes. I liked Janie so much that when she was under some sanction for running away once too often, she told me to sneak in a lighter for her and a few fags, as she wasn't allowed into the courtyard. Luckily they never really frisked me in coming in or out, despite the fact I managed to get in several pencil sharpeners during my time there (the razors inside them were good for cutting). I felt like some prison jimmy; the grass that would earn the respect of the lifers or something. The upshot of that was that Coleen Nolan came and told me off in a really scary Irish way, 'Did you give Janie that lighter. You mustn't give her things like that. I'm serious, do you know what happened the last time she got hold of a lighter? She tried to start a fire.' Her words sent an electric shock of fear straight to my ballbags! I had never really taken the whole ward life seriously until then.

The first weekend home after being on the ward was strange. The house looked really wrong, as if the scale had changed. My nan was hurriedly running about looking after my nephew, Wes. She sort of said, 'Hello,' as if nothing was wrong. I was still attached to my diaries. The ones that I'd obsessed over for the six months previously. A part of me was worried that my dad had snooped through them. He had that ability to really invade your privacy, and that worry was still at the back of my head.

Sadly there wasn't much male attention on the ward. There was a little gonk white boy who smoked loads of weed and was very quiet. Andrew, a boy with Asperger's, terrified me because he said after I'd been with him and Gonk, 'He thinks you're gay. Don't worry I have problems with my sexuality, too.' Such a depressing sentence - *I Have Problems*. Even in my repressed post-bullied, internalised homophobic state, the idea of sexuality being a 'problem' was something I felt deeply saddened by.

One boy I did think I might have a chance with (as he was totally cuckoo) was Mohammed, who arrived at the unit in a full-blown state of psychosis. He imagined himself to be the Statue of Liberty, and that *Team America* had created some special code inside him. He also thought that we believed he was a terrorist. It all got a bit much when he played Evanescence's *My Immortal* in the common room over and over again. I don't quite know what made me think we might be perfect together.

I went from in-patient to day-patient to in-patient again several times. I'd effectively been institutionalised. This was the first bit of real community, social contact and help I'd been given in years. I couldn't give it up. I was stuck in limbo. The moment I showed any signs of recovery, the powers that be (in this case Dr. Cowardly Lion) wanted me out and into the big wide world. This was a prospect that held little appeal for me.

Where would I go? And what would I do with no qualifications? No confidence? No sanity? It was far preferable to cling to this lifeline of regular meals, routine and a captive (if catatonic) audience. People came and went, and new schizophrenics and depressives were added into the mix. Some threw their belongings everywhere, others smashed their faces in mirrors and all the while I still thought this would be the best place for me. My parents had got used to the idea of me being there and didn't really visit me anymore because of the fact that they still got to see me at weekends.

Dr. Cohn, who I continued to see, guessed it out of me, after she'd stated, 'Was it because you were gay?' I replied with an unsure, 'Yes,' and yet her reaction was one of indifference. I actually felt so relieved when she wanted to talk about it at great length, even after I had experienced such difficulty in telling her.

I finally left the ward, or was forcibly ejected, with a pocket full of Prozac, and the prospect of indefinite income support. But Dr. Cohn's training had come to an end after five months, even though we were meant to have had twelve together. Dr. Sayed had also left, and both had been replaced by a small German female shrink with a ridiculous name, and a male psychologist who was going to do CBT with me. Dr. Cohn said, 'Oh I did tell him what you said about your sexuality, because it took you so long to tell me,' which had the effect of annoying me. I was particularly antagonistic towards him and the process, but only because I had so enjoyed the previous one. I also think with hindsight that I do have a tendency to be jealous of other men's physicality, especially if I find it attractive.

Turning eighteen, I left the Adolescent Community Mental Health Team and moved to the adult one, and my new consultant was - and this is the truth - if this were a character in a novel you'd think the author was only capable of limited invention - his name was Dr. Brain, Dr. Paul Brain.

P. Brain.

I was open about talking of my sexuality to him. Old pea brain. It seemed to go past unnoticed. He felt the best course of action was group therapy. 'Young people's' group therapy. That's 18-25. The waiting list was a year, and I was particularly apprehensive about going, worrying that I might get set upon or laughed at. I was also half hoping there would be a fit boy there.

During the interim I did go off the rails once again and had to be rushed to A&E once, where I was particularly antagonistic to the duty doctor, having a go at him, literally just for being a Doctor. 'Homosexuality used to be a mental illness till 1981, didn't it, so maybe what I have will be discounted one day?' Piss poor argument, but it is always a fact I like to use with mental health professionals as it gives a perspective to the limitations of their understanding on matters of what is normal human behaviour.

Neither of my assumptions came to fruition, as I forgot that other people there came for a reason too. It took two sessions before the girl who started with me finally said, 'Can I ask you a question?' That's always how they start it. Why can't they just assume it? It would be so much less hassle.

I said, 'Yeeees,' and of course she asked, 'Are you gay?'

I said, 'What, like your mum?'

But then finally, with doleful resignation, I replied...
'Yes.'

Once it was cleared up, it transpired that her entire reason for asking was that a gay friend of hers had supposedly shared some of the same mannerisms as me, which irritated me profoundly.

The only thing I could sense was that the group leader was a little careful when talking about gay issues, but too careful, as if trying to be politically correct because she didn't really know what she was talking about. I consequently had a lot of unnecessary fun suggesting that she was homophobic, even though she obviously wasn't, and it became easy to bring it to a normal issue of equality, as much as suggesting that one might have problems with one's heterosexuality.

An important turning point, which coincided with leaving Aquarius for good, was that we moved a few miles up the road from Rosehill to the leafy, quiet and essentially wholesome Merton Park. Although there had been a murder of a tramp in the disused nursery school, an honour killing next door (they cut her up and put her in a suitcase and took her to Birmingham) and a woman who somehow commanded the obsessive ardour of a local weirdo who worked in the launderette and had stabbed her fourteen times in the head at the Merton Park tram stop – Although it had a higher death count than Midsomer… our new home was an idyll compared to Rosehill.

It was time for me to spread my legs and try some new things.

7.
NANCY

'I sometimes hold it half a sin
To put in words the grief I feel;
For words, like Nature, half reveal
And half conceal the Soul within.

But, for the unquiet heart and brain,
A use in measured language lies;
The sad mechanic exercise,
Like dull narcotics, numbing pain.

In words, like weeds, I'll wrap me o'er,
Like coarsest clothes against the cold:
But that large grief which these enfold
Is given in outline and no more.'

Alfred Lord Tennyson, In Memoriam

The reason for those three illustrious quatrains is to commemorate the fact that my nan's grandfather was head gardener to Alfred Lord Tennyson at his Isle of Wight home, where he was often spotted in his cape, wandering the grounds, his hands clasped, mumbling his old poems to himself.

There was a seismic shift in the family when my nan died in 2005. She was the centre of our universe. It was completely unexpected, too, as she was ostensibly as strong as an ox. It hit everyone very hard.

She was born in 1925, worked for the ICI during the war, and spent most of her adult life looking after her children and husband, reciting the stories of her family history with incredible wit and insight.

This chapter is not only about my nan, though. It's also about the effect of the sudden loss of someone, and the permanent grief it can leave you with.

TUESDAY 30TH AUGUST 2005

In All Bar One for 'lunch; with Mr. H, smoked salmon bagels, chocolate cheesecake and two cups of coffee; he paid. He mentioned my blank 'E' in English Lit, and said Carslake Boys High School (apart from a select few) were all 'Fucking Arseholes'.

Did an afternoon 1.30 – 4.30pm at Princess Alice (Charity Shop). This ancient old queen with a funny mouth called Keith volunteers there, and says 'Old Son'. Woo and Jay, two Korean girls, helped. A crazy bloke called Anthony Whittaker (written on his walking stick) came into the staff bit, demanding his dead wife's silk blouses. 'It's appalling. I've only been out the hospital two hours'.

Got home to hear news of nan. Nancy, my only nan (maternal), has gone into hospital. I fear the worst. She fell over in Tesco's,[27] and they have discovered that there is a high amount of potassium in her kidneys. When Nanny Wendy (paternal) went in, they said, 'It'll be alright', and she died. I can't imagine how she's coping. I want to rush to her side and

---

27 She was, in fact, hit hard with a trolley in her side by a rushing shopper, which caused her to break her hip in the subsequent fall.

hug her and kiss her, but I'm here, unable to do anything for her. I've got that leaving dinner at NRG (the gay youth group) for James tomorrow. I'd rather see nan. But the family all say, 'Oh no... go!' They say she'll only be there for a fortnight. Vicky was with her. I keep trying to tell myself that it will be alright. Mum says, 'Life goes on'.

WEDNESDAY 31ST AUGUST 2005

In Pizza Express with the remnants of NRG. Antonio says to James, 'If you're straight, then my Mother's a virgin'. Talked to Matthew at the bus stop, might get together, but... I don't know. He's sweet, but will only be friends, I reckon.

Nan's got her bed, and her kidneys haven't packed up, but they're doing tests for something, so she's not all clear.

THURSDAY 1ST SEPTEMBER 2005

Saw nan in hospital, she looks okay. Just goes on about what everyone else should be doing. She seems happy in herself, nothing shocking in the medical report that she refuses to read. It's tearing my soul apart, to think of her ill, and not knowing if it'll be a long stay, but she's 80, had such a good long run together... What am I saying? Anyway, 'Nan'll be fine,' is my mantra. I even prayed for her! No, I have been!

At night, and at fleeting moments in the day, these morbid thoughts and images.

FRIDAY 2ND SEPTEMBER 2005

Nan now in Renal ward. I feel numb, stiff, achey, ill.

My sister came round at half seven because of an argument with the Pig. She said, 'I don't want nan to die'. I felt all scared inside. That same sinking feeling I got in my stomach when I was little. But she's Not at death's door.

Nan said to mum when she went up tonight, 'Oh, when is Simon coming? He's so affectionate.' The news of this made me want to cry, but I haven't shed a tear yet.

I don't like the thought of nan in hospital. Emma wept. She cried so much. Sue was a nice assuring voice. Will see her on Tuesday. I must remain optimistic. But I don't know how bad she is. Aunt Vi was planning to go to Egypt for the week on Sunday, but I don't think she's going now.

Nan was born on the 31st of October 1925. Nan asked the nurse if she'd still be in the hospital for her birthday. The nurse said she'd be out by then. But… oh, I dread to think of the outcome of all this.

Things all seem to be carrying on as usual.

Emma felt guilty for crying in front of me.

WEDNESDAY 7TH SEPTEMBER 2005

11.50am – 'Nan died'. Mum told me. She woke me at 3am yesterday morning. Nan passed on at quarter to two. I'd been crying buckets, wailing like a banshee on Saturday and Sunday when Nan was getting worse. She was sound asleep apart from waking once. She couldn't talk.

I feel calm and resolved, but everyone's finding it hard, obviously. I've been at Vi's since Saturday. I just popped back here to be on my own. I went to see Ali (my therapist) on Tuesday, with Vicky. I was like a zombie. Granddad seems okay. My estranged Uncle Kevin has come back into the fold since Saturday, and his wife Helen drove us to Sutton Hospital. I've just come back from there now, saw Dr. Burp. She's going to refer me for bereavement counselling.

I'm going to be fine. I'm going to be everyone's shoulder to cry on and help out, whenever and wherever.

I'm still going to call nan's house, 'Nan's'.

I suppose they will want to sort out funeral arrangements next.

THURSDAY 8TH SEPTEMBER 2005

The funeral is going to be held on Tuesday 20th at 10am. Nan is going to be cremated, then her ashes are going to be buried in her mother's grave.

FRIDAY 9TH SEPTEMBER 2005

My mind is a blank. I don't know what to put down. Is there anything *to* put down? I don't want to burden my grieving family with my tedious woes. Keep strong for her memory. Still it hasn't hit me, cause I'm not letting it.

I've got to start writing my 'speech' for the funeral.

SATURDAY 10TH SEPTEMBER 2005

Granddad took to his bed today, after having what Vicky described as a 'panic attack'.

I've got the gist of my speech worked out, but still don't want to think about it. I've been distracting myself constantly. I've been trying to write, but even before pen gets to paper, I retire, deciding that there is absolutely no point whatsoever in doing it. Gorgeous Italian (I think) guy, young, muscly, little orange vest etc. on train and an equally gorgeous black guy on the way home.

I suppose soon I'll be sitting in the park by the *Marquis of Lorne* on Haydons Road, waiting for a gay guy to come out and clock me, take me home, rape and murder me…

It would be wonderful to write 70,000 words about Nancy's life, rather than my own. It's odd this chapter as I've included the most scant of details about one of the most important women in my life.

In all honesty, 11 years on, it's still just as painful to think about her and the fact that I will never see her again. A null, a void, something so huge and cosmic, that it just renders a nothing between my ears. I can't imagine what she'd think to read this book. The comments about fancying men would've resulted in a heavy friendly chuckle followed by a hacking cough. She'd then venture off down side-paths retelling me the story of how she narrowly avoided missing the bomb that was dropped by the Luftwaffe at the top of West Sutton because she stayed late that night at the Bug Hutch Picturehouse to watch Elizabeth and Essex a second time. I feel it is the best anecdote in the Universe, to reveal that the existence of my mother, my sister and myself is entirely reliant on that charismatic performance from Bette Davies.

Stories like that and a million others were told me by my nan. One day I shall come back, yes, one day, and write about her.

Until then there must be no tears, no anxieties… and if you get my reference, you're one handsome organism.

8.
YOOF GROUPS

'Henceforth I'll bear affliction till it do cry out itself.'

King Lear, Act IV, Scene VI

Perhaps it's about time to detail the loss of my virginity.

As good a time as any, although some gay men, or 'men who sleep with men' (or 'denial') sometimes like to term the loss of their virginity in stages. If they top, that's one stage, then when they bottom (more special) then that's another balloon knot in the pink hankie.

As the innocent that I was (and still am in many ways) this reminiscence details the beginnings of my first real affectionate boy-on-boy action, but the actual act, which was mostly a slurping and sucking affair, could hardly be called a loss of virginity by anyone's standards. To some Presidents of the United States it's not even considered a sexual act at all. But there we are.

To the reminiscence, then...

'Yish', a Singaporean 24 year old who was travelling around Europe, came to NRG Central on this particular Thursday to 'hang out'. I shook his hand when he introduced himself, but didn't talk much to him, as I was focused on Rosanne. She is so funny and clever and all the rest of it, but has just had a bad time with a miscarriage, and also has to live in a stinking Croydon B&B, history of overdosing, etc. etc.

Anyway, we had a little jaunt round London, just aimlessly wandering: Me, Dan, Mikey, Yish, Keith, Rosanne. Yish was asking for all our e-mail addresses. I gave mine, thinking nothing of it.

Rosanne said to me on the train back to Waterloo, 'Oooh that Yisheng really fancies Keith, it's so obvious. But he's sixteen, and Yish is 24.'

Well, that didn't stop what happened.

It had been on the cards since Sunday evening.

It started out as something innocent.

We had met up at Waterloo Station on Sunday afternoon, and had caught the tube to Oxford Circus. I was leading Yish towards Old Compton Street. He unwittingly followed. We had coffee, walked round the block back to the street and had dinner. I was doing my self-deprecating depressing loser routine. He kept dropping hints, saying, 'Oh, you're so handsome'. He then said, 'Why don't we meet up at mine... or yours?' I asked *faux naïve* but sounded like I was taking the piss. 'Oh, *why?*' He did this little flirty smile and replied, 'You know why'. My blood instantly went cold at the proposition, resulting in Monday's 'meet up' not having the desired effect.

He met me at Wimbledon Station 10am on Monday morning, and we walked back to mine (knowing that Ma and Pa would be out at work). Despite the opportunity, nothing happened. Every time he so much as looked at me, I recoiled in horror. He suggested putting the telly on, and we were watching a 'Theory of Everything' programme on Channel 4, and these crap CGIs of atoms, blah blah blah...

I then told him I was nervous because I was a virgin and had not so much as had one snog in my entire life. He immediately tried to remedy this, but I pulled away. He wasn't annoyed though, and just commented that maybe it was the fact that we were in my flat. He said he fancied me, he liked my hair, and would love to 'shag me senseless'.

Later that day when I was on my own again my mind started going into overdrive at the thought that there was someone who found me attractive and wanted to sleep with me. I texted him saying sorry I was so frigid, and that I would meet him at his place the next day.

At twenty past two that afternoon I got off at Finchley Road Tube Station, met up with Yish. He was wearing a *Nike* vest jacket. We walked to where he was staying (expensive posh flat that a friend of the family, Mr. Jackson, owned). Door number D. I walked into the living room and he immediately went to kiss me. I let him. He tried to get his tongue in my mouth but I pulled away. He said, 'Come with me to the bedroom.' I said, nervously, 'You'll have to drag me there,' but followed him in. I sat on the edge of the unmade double bed. He put a wad of tissues on the desk and sat next to me.

'What are THOSE for?' I demanded, pointing in horror.

'Just in case. Things tend to get a bit messy,' he said sweetly.

I was grossed out. But I soon relaxed into it.

He was very sweet. It was fun, and nothing like I had imagined. Just being naked with another man was wonderful. His cock was a bit disappointing but easy to put in my mouth.

The kissing and hugging was the best bit. I liked him rubbing his hands over my body and I liked doing it back. He said he liked the scars on my arm, which was sweet, but odd. And yes it did get messy. His cum face was weird.

There you are - wasn't that fun!

A merry time was had. I was so excited and even relieved that I'd done the act, rather than getting too worried about deconstructing the whole thing.

Youth group shenanigans were my main outlet after leaving hospital, and going to LGBT youth groups was a great way to socialise. The problem was, I had been out of the 'socialising normally with groups of teenagers' loop for a long time. I was now acting weird and my hardened persona was constantly self-deprecating, still the class clown, but all the jokes were at my own expense. It was a suffocating defence mechanism.

Being the new boy, I flourished at first. I loved talking to the group leaders and even fancied a few of them (daddy issues). I found all the guys sexy, though they didn't really show any interest in me. They didn't explain clearly that they were interested in me, though I found out later that some were, which was a bit annoying in retrospect. I started going to a comfy little place in Waterloo with the first youth group. It was all rather well-mannered, and this was where I met Rosanne, who became a very close friend. She was a bit of a ditz, this stocky black Thelma from Scooby-Doo pansexual and ADD social whirlwind. It was quite a heady time being in her orbit. She popped in and out in those early years. Sometimes we'd go for a coffee in Croydon, though often she'd turn up a few hours late and be susceptible to outbursts of insane unexplained anger.

One social group paved the way for another, and somehow I started going to a group in Greenwich. The first main do was a Halloween party, something which I didn't dress up for. I'm already monstrous enough, I thought at the time. I want to now go back and give myself a massive slap in the face.

It was there that boys like Z (he's not getting the oxygen of publicity, because if he did, we'd all suffocate!) and Nate and Mica who were interested in me, made themselves known. Nate had blue lipstick on and cerebral palsy, beautiful brown eyes and a cockney patter. My heart fluttered instantly. Mica had some Greek in him, I think, and nice abs, so that was enough.

It was a fun night. I relegated myself to the back door to smoke as many Mayfair KingSize as possible.

One thing I did for a while was to pretend to have some sort of hand abnormality. This was copied from Dennis Potter's psoriatic arthropathy, where his hands literally buckled into crippled, swollen boxing gloves, all gnarled, and he'd have to smoke between thumb and clump. This is what I was doing, anyway. I spent all evening with my hands clamped into clenched fists. I kept up this pretence quite a lot. People believed me (well perhaps they didn't, but I still liked doing it).

The party migrated to this Irish guy's place. I don't really want to dispense names or accounts too thoroughly as it could result in criminal prosecution which would never do, would it? We don't want this book to become a handout in a court room do we? (although it *would* put the sales up… morally tricky territory)

So let's call him Uncle O'Grimacy, or Grimacy for short, as that was the name of Grimace's Irish uncle (Grimace, if you don't know, was the purple blob, the anthropomorphised taste-bud used in the McDonald's advertisements from around 1970-1990, I think). Grimacy was this flabby, squat guy with curly hair and huge eyes. Like saucers they was!

A group of us went on this long extended walk around Greenwich, into the tunnel that goes under the Thames, up by the Cutty Sark (pre-fire). All that. A lot of the time Mica was trying to grab me, Nate was trying to chat to me and Z was chucking compliments at me. Didn't take the hint to any of that.

Grimacy invited us all back across London to the flat for some all-night boozing, and I went along. There were lesbians there and everything, although the one I was friendly with the most was called a Butternut Squash, which really wasn't fair on her. So the night went on. I even went for a lie-down on Grimacy's bed, and Mica came and laid by me. Still, I didn't take the hint. Woe'st!

I went out for a cigarette to the balcony, which was covered in dried dog-shit from a little ratty pooch he had (oh it's all coming back to me now, like that awful Celine Dion song, the name of which escapes me). I looked across at the view of a rough part of west London, trying to avoid the crusty fecal matter. Grimacy joined me. He started talking in this quasi-philosophical way: 'Don't you feel that there are connections, that two people could sense something great in one another.' Such utter bollocks. I sucked at the filter knowingly. He'd been talking to people on the balcony all evening. His stage for such moments.

I feel by writing this down I have somehow opened a window into the past, and that I am seeing it unfold again in real-time, powerless to do anything. Some fun writing this malarkey, but oh, but oh, oh, oh, but oh… as the late Rik Mayall would say, it is silly. It's happened. I could if I wanted rewrite it and tell Grimacy to fuck off and that he was a slimy little toad, and then go and suck on someone else's toadstool. Yes, I'm gonna go and slurp on Mica's doner kebab. But no, back to the moment...

I was hypnotised by Grimacy's words, and I snuggled under a blanket with him and snogged his big wet mouth. We were caught snogging in the kitchen by Z, who looked as if he had walked in on someone transmogrifying into a giant welted stink-bug. He looked utterly disgusted.

Grimacy seemed to almost enjoy the disgust Z displayed. Was this all a game to all these experienced gay boys? I didn't even find him attractive. I fancied Mica or Nate, even Z, even though he was a bit too skinny and described his dick as being like a pencil, He displayed an utter middle-class arrogant contempt for everyone and everything.

People were a bit shocked. I ended up with Grimacy. I 'went out' with him for a month. Not that we really went out anywhere. Not on his terms, despite all his declarations of love, These weren't really declarations. He used to say, 'I'm not in love with you, but I'm falling.' He'd often go on about the fact that he'd been raped once. When I bummed him he tried to get away from me and then he'd say, 'You've got to make me stay and keep doing it'. There were all these rumours about him being dodgy during that month. I mean he was hardly a charmer. He once drew me a calligraphied thing with 'Love' written on it. That was the extent of his selflessness. He also bought me a Morley's.

Yes, the rumours, which were confirmed by a friend who was witness to this shocking event, was that Grimacy liked to spike people's drinks. I guess he realised I had very little self-control or ability to stop someone fucking me if they wanted to (even if I didn't want it and said so) that he didn't really bother with me. Although, thinking back now, there were times when I felt exceptionally light headed and strange and had to lie down in his flat.

There was a tale doing the rounds about this Emo boy who went over to Grimacy's for the evening with a sane associate who flared up this spiking scenario to the group. Allegedly, drinks were handed round and Emo went all weird and had to lie down. The sane boy left shortly after, feeling a little drunk and uncomfortable with Grimacy's weird advances. What transpired from Emo was that Grimacy raped him. Someone tried to warn me at the youth group but I didn't want to know. 'Like most ugly people I prefer to be left in the dark,' I retorted to the dissenters before storming out.

The whole Grimacy chapter was rather unpleasant. I'd always have to go to his grotty little flat on the estate. We'd do very little, and then maybe have sex. I put up with it long enough so I could lose my virginity (step 2). I was so obsessed with the thought that all I had to do was lose it and then I'd have grown up! Like some magical pork-amulet going up my jacksee was going to unleash wisdom.

The first time was rather odd. We drank from specific glasses (hello…) and I recall dimly having my arms tied to the bed. He lubed me up. I think he rimmed me. It's all a bit blurry. Then he pumped his stubby fat chode in my starfish for a little while. It was rather dull, and I think he came, but I never really knew to be honest. I certainly didn't cum. It was about as erotic as Anne Robinson's neck.

I staggered home weak-legged and weak-headed after that. I only saw him one more time on New Year's Day 2006. He was in a complete daze for some reason. I tried to talk to him encouragingly but he was monosyllabic. There were cigarette butts of a different brand to his in the ashtray, and I went all Eastenders on him and asked, 'Whose are these?' He said with a smirk, 'It's none of your business'.

It soon dawned on me that the whole situation was not the way a good, healthy relationship worked. I had always known that, but in the back of the head, I had so little self-worth at that time, and no real guidance of a relationship, other than the ones I'd already seen in my life. Ironically Grimacy tried to contact me a year later, professing his love over and over again. I just replied, 'If you contact me again I shall be forced to inform the police. You drink-spiking cunt'.

*   *   *

One paranoid upshot from that sticky little affair was that I was convinced I'd contracted HIV. This was due to

a) Z making some rude comment over the phone about it when I spoke to him and

b) I was so ignorant of the virus, I just thought if I had unprotected sex with a gay man it's 99.99% likely I'm going to get it.

This resulted in a long wait at St. Thomas's STI clinic followed by a further fourteen days of agony. A long anxious fortnight ensued such silliness. Of course it was negative.

All of these teenage fumblings to most people are tedious and embarrassing, and, I think, common. I think mine also lacked a very important dimension. For some reason I never really went for guys that I actually fancied. In fact I didn't go for guys at all, in the sense that I didn't ask them out. I just hung around in the vicinity and waited for guys to pick me up. I also gave off the vibe of being sad, lonely and desperate, as well as having zilch self-esteem. I was, however, good-looking, young and skinny. If only I'd known. I could've had as much fun as I'd wanted… But there we are! Passive goings on with guys who fancied me. I can still count on both hands the number of men I've had proper sexual encounters with. Actually, I'd rather not think about it haha!. This was obviously a trait of the latterly diagnosed Emotionally Unstable Personality Disorder.

Grimacy wasn't the only misstep, though, when it came to my gentlemen suitors. There was also a long-haired boy I'll call Paul. He had eyes that were of different colours, like Bowie, and who dressed like some avant-garde queer dandy. He had long, perfectly manicured nails, painted with exquisite designs. His mouth was always turned into a strange curl, and he had a permanent squint. He was one of the boys that talked to me in the group. Not very much, just an odd word here and there. I think he bought me a box of maltesers once around Christmas. (I might have imagined that) I don't want to make it sound like he was capable of compassion or being caring, because he wasn't.

For some reason, perhaps pity, my own lack of imagination or will, I went home with him one evening. I sat up with him for hours as he talked about his mother, going to therapy with her, how they described her as a 'whore' in the notes; how he had to get away from them; how he rolled around on the floor sexually with his obese cousin. He then spent a good couple of hours going on about vacuum cleaners he liked, the different types and models, and even talked me through a catalogue. Perhaps it was sleep deprivation, but I ended up in bed with him, although the look of his genitals (unwashed) were like a wilted red chilli-pepper. When I was finally lying on top of him, I noticed that he actually had a nice body, with his face untense and, in the moonlight, he looked quite beautiful. He spoke more slowly and calmly too. For that moment he seemed relaxed and happy.

Most of the time before and especially the time after he was the opposite of those things. He said, 'It's because I'm with you'. I think I told him a lot of romantic nonsense, which I probably shouldn't have. We even shared a bath. Looking back it was quite sweet, if a little strange. I had to leave him in the end, as I was knackered. As I went to leave, he asked 'Can I have some money for the laundry? Seven pounds please,' in a slightly menacing tone. So without question, I gave it to him! I enquired about the tomatoes he had growing underneath his boiler. He told me they were from 'human composting'. I shudder now at the thought that he grew his own with fertiliser made from his own shit.

For me, that autistic spectrum evening with Paul was a one time thing. There were some nice moments, but I didn't see us ever being much else than friends. I tried to explain this to him time and time again, but he didn't seem to understand. I took him flowers and explained. He finally seemed to take it in, and we hugged on the bed and watched *The Young Ones*. But the next time I went, it was back to square one. The flowers I gave him were in exactly the same position in the sink, dead! I did feel for Paul. However, my condition and his condition mingled together was no cocktail, in any sense, so it turned into this protracted duel of separation and kinship, with no defined boundaries or understanding.

Unfortunately I have since repeated this pattern with

a guy with Aspergers' at Uni. Yes autism thunder really does strike twice. And it wasn't really the fact that he had autism that was a problem. I made that allowance in the way we interacted. He was actually a cunt separate to that. He started following me home on the train, ringing my home-phone and mobile all the time. I n the end I had to just avoid both him and going to the group. It was a bit of an annoyance. He did keep rearing his head over the next year or two, still worryingly obsessed, and with the same preoccupations. What upset me was that people were mean to him and ignored him. He was a strange boy, a rude one, but not really that different from the rest of us. We were all bitches in that youth group. All we had over him was a false veneer of social boundaries. It's a dubious advantage when all is said and done.

I wonder what became of him?

A lot of my personal time was now spent on the MSN messenger, then in its heyday. I reached a perfect paradigm. I'd spend hours talking to strangers in chat rooms as I smoked menthol cigarettes and drank pints of milk. When the self-loathing got too much, I'd burn or cut myself.

My main social outlet was Thingbox and (the now defunct) MSN, where I managed to talk to any amount of interesting people. There are friendships I made and lost online that were incredibly intense. I guess the reality of them would have spoiled it. There was this guy called James, who was amazing. He was Mancunian-Japanese - what a gorgeous mix!. He was pretty, posh and clever and loved chatting to me. He had a girlfriend, but was such an exhibitionist! He loved to show off his body, and masturbate on cam for me. A straight boy (supposedly) who would give himself to me.

There is this whole 'winning the love of a straight man'

fantasy which pervades a certain type in the (loosely termed) gay community (which is a bit like saying the female community or the consumptive community). The whole 'I want a straight man to love me', seems on the surface to be some internalised homophobia, suggesting somehow that other gay men are less attractive because they self-identify as gay. There was perhaps then some truth in it, because the amount of societal signifying and personal abuse I'd received, well it rubbed off, and not in a fun way. But deeper than that, my theory about wanting a straight guy isn't all negative. I think the fantasy comes from the idea of self-sacrifice. If a man who does not normally find any man attractive, finds you attractive, that is (1) utter loyal and unconditional devotion and suggests (2) he will give up the life he knows and understands just for you… You're a unique interest. 1 in 6 billion.

Also, there is the stigma he will have to undertake just to be with you. Perhaps he still isn't attracted to men in a sexual way, but he loves you so much, he'll do it just for you. I feel this is the root of the deep fantasy. It's total adoration, something I guess as a social outcast you would want. James was a bit like this. He was pretty, he had a girlfriend, but he'd always be so kind to me. You could argue that he was a closet case, or bi, or that sexuality is a lot more fluid than Gay/Straight/Bi and so on… If we were being rational, I'd go with the third option. But surely if people are allowed to belief in something as ridiculous as God, then we should all be allowed to have faith in the idea that a straight man may occasionally deign to give you an award-winning blow-job.

Yes, James was a sweet boy. He so-ooh wanted to meet me. He'd put up with my self-deprecating. He'd put up with anything. He said, 'Come to Oxford. I'll put you up. You can stay in my bed. We can hug, and if anything happens, it happens.' Which was all rather exciting. Poor bitch of a girlfriend, though, alas! It never happened, not unlike how in my naivete, I thought meeting in 'Oxford' meant Oxford Street on the Bakerloo Line, and not the seat of that prestigious University. Shame.

Halcyon reminiscences aside, I was having quite a lot of fun too, especially with my friend Rosanne. We'd often have creative jaunts hither and thither. One of the greatest qualities of any friendship, and one I hold very highly, is the ability to make and to be made to laugh. Rosanne and I have always had that in spades. She (by her own admission) can be an infuriating utter nonsense of a person, but still, no matter how silly she gets (and she has got very silly over the years) I have always find myself regularly sucked back into her orbit.

All this socialising was in lieu of regular medical intervention.

At this point there came a boy that I actually had feelings for and Wanted to sleep with. No, surely not? Surely I didn't have the potential for such a thing. But wait. This was something new. It was Nate, the boy who had first introduced himself at Greenwich. The boy with the blue lipstick and the palsy. The cheeky chappy cockney lad. There was something sweet about him, but annoyingly he was a headfuck from beginning to finish.

I was completely besotted with him. He fancied me, I thought, but it was never the right time. He was always with someone. If it wasn't one boy it was another. I befriended him, of course, but the lack of reciprocation was agonising. Of course this sent me off the rails. Despite the fluoxetine (or whatever drug I was on at the time) coursing through my veins, I was livid that he wasn't making a move on me. I broke down in front of the staff at the youth group one afternoon, privately, after he'd fucked off with some other boy. I was taken to A&E and then taxied by the duty doctor's orders back to Springfield, where I was put on the adult ward until I could be assessed. There I was having a crying fit episode of spectacular proportions, and one in which I couldn't get a grip. I used the phone on the ward (which was nothing like Aquarius) to ring Belinda, my old teacher from Drapers, who I'd become a bit chummy with. I was just blathering on a load of rubbish to her down the line, 'I cut my ear shaving and am wearing this fucking stupid plaster on my ear.'

'Well if you were aiming for your wrist, you missed,' came her pithy reply. Her joke made me giggle, and that, dear friends, is the power of real friendship. She knew the sane and sorted Simon underneath's sick and twisted humour would respond, and it did. I snapped out of it. I knew deep down I didn't need another hospital stay.

I saw adults racked with illness. A man kept coming up to me and asking me if I was Dr. Potter. I went into the common room and a woman was playing a harp to a captive audience and then told an anecdote to the wall about the time she met David Bowie. I demanded to see the doctor and have him let me go home. Luckily I knew the necessary jargon to convince them that I was no risk to myself and that I wanted to leave. It was about midnight at this point and my poor parents had to come and pick me up. They weren't best pleased. If only we knew then what we know now about my condition, it would've been a lot easier. The poor bastards, having to put up with all of that.

The whole Nate affair wasn't much of a success. I remember the joy of finally getting to go on a date with him. By this point his hair was purple, his jeans were baggy and his eyes were supernovas. We went to see the film *Capote* at the Prince Charles Cinema in Leicester Square, and were soon groping each others cocks in the back seat. We just wanted to do each other there and then under the beady eyes of Philip Seymour Hoffman. I don't think we'd even kissed at that point.

After that, I took him to Pizza Hut and I hit upon the very clever trick of ordering one bottomless coke between the pair of us with two straws. Romantic and thrifty. He kept asking if he could come home with me. 'I don't eat much and I can sleep in the fridge,' was his cute phrase. I texted it to my mum. It was a bit cramped at home, in a good way, as Emma had finally left Pig and was staying at ours whilst she found something better. Luckily Mother allowed Nate to come and stay.

We snogged like crazy all the way back on the 156 as it trundled down Lavender Hill towards home. One woman tapped us on the shoulder and said, 'Don't let the passion fade!' We took a breath to reply that we wouldn't. 'How long have you been going out?' she said, to which Nate replied, 'We're not'. This shattered my oldy-worldy sensibilities.

The sex was rubbish. No, it was worse than rubbish. Just saying it's 'rubbish' gives the suggestion that there was some possibility in some other parallel universe that it could've been good. No chance. I was nervous as fuck, so I *WAS* rubbish (with the considered probability that I would improve over time) but Nate was so selfish. He just laid back and I had to do the old Monica Lewinsky (which of course I am not averse to). Nate's penis was a very beautiful, big and circumcised one. What upset me was that as soon as he came, he was immediately distracted by things like what DVDs I had. He had no concern whether I might want to get off or anything.

The next morning the same scenario repeated itself. Then he wanted to watch *Misery* (how fucking apt!). I so wanted him to kiss me like we had the previous night. I just hung by him all day, in the hope he'd hug me or kiss me again. NOPE. We parted our separate ways at South Wimbledon Tube, where he promised to bum me (if I was lucky) next week. He never kept that promise. Still I kept trying to get in touch with him sporadically over the next year or two, to little or no avail. In recent years as my adoration for him has waned, I see him more for what he is. Which isn't great.

After that incident and the Paul stalking I decided to give the youth group a wide berth, and spend more time online.

* * *

Now let me introduce you to some young gay men that give the community a good name. Shining beacons of this generation's finest. James, Robert and sometimes Jack, and sometimes a lot of other hangers-on, formed a little coterie of friendships when I started to go to the youth groups again in late 2006.

I was apprehensive about going again because I was worried I'd bump into Paul, which of course I did on the very first week, but he kept himself to himself, oddly, just staring at me from the corner, his discoloured pupils carrying a jaindiced look of disdain. I remember he called me 'incestuous and vain' once for not responding to his advances. I knew what the second term was, but I always thought incestuous was something to do with gauging your eyes out after getting a boner over your mum (Greek style). I wonder if it has any other connotations? (Quick... to the Websters...) Apparently the other meaning is 'excessively close and resistant to outside influence.' Which surely doesn't fit the bill? Anyway there is no point crying over spilt crazy now is there?

The new Croydon social group was a major laugh. There were acting students there like Jo, or sixth formers like James and Robert, who were all so normal. Of course I fancied all the weird boys like the Geordie lad, who once accidentally bit his own tongue off and had to have it sewn back on. Then there was another guy, whose name I can't even remember, a middle class creative who fancied Robert, the permanently cheery blonde one. Everyone fancied him, though Robert fancied James who fancied the group leader who fancied the other group leader who fancied me who fancied the Geordie who fancied Jack who fancied no-one in the group because he'd already managed to get off with most of his class and was now into cruising, which we were all much too pussy-assed to do ourselves (still are).

What was great about this new Croydon entourage, was (apart from the fact that it was in Croydon) that it meant I finally had an accepting social group, that was healthy and safe and who would invite me to hang out with them! Of course I'd be a self-deprecating shit most of the time but I also really had my A game of humour sorted then. I'd work really hard on thinking up lots of funny stuff before I met up, and then exhaust myself in preparation. Funnily enough I wasn't the most fucked up boy there. There was another boy with freckles and very wide nostrils who hung around with us and who was even more annoying. Bless him, he always wore a horrible Del Boy jacket and bullshitted outrageously.

We started spending a lot more time in Crystal Palace, going over the park and enjoying the utterly rubbish hedge maze. Elements of Crystal Palace Park still remind me of some post-apocalyptic environment, especially the big concrete overpass set amongst the foliage that seemed to lead to nowhere. Am I remembering it right? It's been too long… thankfully.

Robert invited outsiders to these sojourns to Crystal Palace. One was Tom, a middle class anglo-chinese type who scorned us all, despite living in Thornton Heath. Rob was very enamoured of him, although I don't think much happened there. Another of Robert's dalliances was this guy who I suppose I shall have to be very secretive about here. We will call him Chipmunk. No, that won't work as there is a low-rent rapper called that. Chip, lets go with Chip. 'Chip' was linked with Rob. That's how I got to know him. He was a queeny type from abroad with a confident attitude and a face like a smashed in Tim Curry. For some reason I started hanging out with him too, despite one of the first things he said to me was that I had a 'great face for radio'.

We bonded over the fact that we liked *The Rocky Horror Picture Show*. What was weird was that Chip was the facilitator of my first real boring boyfriend. Now any fan of *The Goonies* will know that when I describe my first real boyfriend, official boyfriend, as Sloth, you'll know that I'm being a complete cunt. But it is a fair description, as he was not a looker. Sloth was very tall, in his thirties, with a pot belly and gangly extremities. He was Scottish too! Post-modern irony over other races translates well on the page does it not? I met Sloth because Chip knew him through Thingbox, the site for alternative gays. These were just regular gays that thought Gaydar was beneath them, although they all turned out to have Gaydar too (hush my mouth).

I went with Chip to visit Sloth as he was picking up some photos. He lived in a neat little underground flat in Earl's Court that used to be a sex dungeon frequented by none other than Freddie Mercury. Praise be upon him. Sloth flirted with me the first time we met, and unfortunately when men flirt with me, no matter if their warped ears wiggle constantly independently of one another, I'm hooked. The attention is worth its weight in razorblades. I had 0% attraction to him, and, as time went on, that actually went down. He was very kind to me and bought my affection, but he needn't have. I would've been happy with the kind words. I led him on enough so I could spend the evening with him. Chip left us to it. Sloth invited me to a friend's Birthday party in Soho, and he paid for my dinner. Sloth and I, via the imbibing of alcohol, got all flirty. The others at the party couldn't really see why I, a still young, skinny twink (effectively) would want to smear my lips over a Ray Harryhousen (the one who made those stop-motion monsters in things like the original Clash of the Titans and Jason and The Argonauts, think Kraken – I am such a cunt!) creature.

But smear I did. Sloth was sweet (most of the time). He was deeply immature for a man in his thirties, prone to having a go at me, and being quite nasty when he wanted to be. Both his parents had died quite young, so I feel that may have affected him. I was as sympathetic to him as I could be, but he was a lot of hard work - and that coming from me!

I later referred to him as 'a one night stand that lasted

for four months,' and that's the truth. What shocked me the most about this relationship was that during it I found out that Chip, the guy who introduced us, was attracted to underage boys! Now, what does one do with this information? Inform the police straight away? Well it's quite an accusation to make with no proof, so I broached the subject with Sloth, and he said, 'It's not baby fucking,' which made me feel physically ill. What am I *doing* with these people? Who are they? Is society this damaged? I was a naïve 18 year old. I was so out of my depth!

*   *   *

As a coda to this chapter of my life (and this book LOL (that lol is ironic and should be heard in your head voice as such) I managed to kill my association with both men dead in one breakdown. I broke up with Sloth - yes it was I who did the dumping - in a cake shop of all places. I'd gone back to my old ways of menthol cigarettes, self-harm and destructive behaviour.

I went out one night with the middle class toff boy, and we got very, very, *very* drunk! I got pissed in G-A-Y, Old Compton Street's cheapest gay bar/dancy place. I was waiting to be served at the bar with all these desperate men all clinging in huddles to it, who wouldn't let me in. In the end I just heaved my weight into them and they toppled over like dominoes. I managed to step over the huddle and get to the front where the infuriatingly cute bar man said, 'Get out, I'm not serving you'. I just ran from the club, leaving Toff to fend for himself. It was utterly pissing it down with rain, but I was so drunk I felt immune to it.

I broke down on the Millennium Bridge, and tried to

find someone in my phonebook to call. Sloth came up first. I cried down the phone to him for help, as I was in such a mess, and hoped we could get back together or something. He sounded pleased I was in such a mess, and wasn't really interested in helping me at all. Actually, that's not really fair. He said something comforting, but was unable to help. Amounts to same thing, really.

The only other option in my phone was Chip. I went to his place where I was a swirling whirling dervish. I couldn't really lay down. I was throwing myself at him, which was as hopeless as it was desperate. I think at the time that I was getting drunk a lot, as Chip once had to rescue me from drinking two bottles of red wine, which I ended up projectile vomiting half of all over Embankment Station.

Being in Chip's flat sickened me. The whole situation sickened me. I went to the kitchen and grabbed a serated knife used to cut beef off the joint and took it to the bathroom. I ran it along my arms and sawed them a bit, but the knife was blunt. I still managed to cut myself enough to feel some satisfaction. I put my shirt back on so the blood would soak into the sleeve. I laid beside Chip as he snored, till about 5am, when I knew I could get the first tube home. The last thing he ever wrote to me was, 'There is blood all over my bathroom!'

I never contacted him again.

9.

PARASITES, FLATS AND COLLEGE

'Yet each man kills the thing he loves
By each let this be heard
Some do it with a bitter look
Some with a flattering word
The coward does it with a kiss
The brave man with a sword'

Oscar Wilde, The Ballad of Reading Gaol

Even though Sloth and Chip were out of my life, I still used Thingbox (an indie-boy gay facebook with forums, and a lot of trolling). I mean a lot. *A lot!*

What amuses me is that the sequence of many of the significant relationships in my life wouldn't be what it is if I'd never floated without direction through the previous ones… 'Everything in your life happens for a reason,' and all that crap. Everything has a knock on effect. Yes, that's the first law of the bleeding obvious. And I guess we console ourselves with the idea that suffering through bad stuff is worthwhile because we'll end up with the good stuff. Possibly. The philosophy of the terminally inept.

But it was through Thingbox that I ended up meeting Parasite. A beanie-hat wearing, bespectacled boy in his late twenties, he looked a little bit like a bird that had just minutes previously hatched its way out of the egg. That or Charles

Hawtrey. Again 0% attraction.

Before we get into all that, let me 'tent-peg' you so you're more aware of where we are…

It's 2007, Gordon Brown has finally been allowed to become Prime-Minister, and unfortunately for him, hasn't called a snap election. Things are just ticking along as per usual. For anything else that was going on in 2007, why don't you Wikipedia '2007'? I'll wait a bit while you do that.

Done? Good. Hooray!

I'd finally been referred for Group Therapy, which was a strange experience, especially as our group facilitator Flav was one of those many soulless twenty-first century blank page leaders who never allowed herself to act like a human being. Consequently we took the piss out of her something rotten, which she interpreted as transference (ie. we were really taking the piss out of ourselves). I did manage to make her laugh sometimes though, as is my wont with Mental Health Professionals. It's just something I like to do. It's all very confidential what happens in those sessions, so it wouldn't be fair to detail it without some heavy fictionalisation (which has been going on the whole time during this book) but I've already fictionalised it an as yet unproduced stageplay, so should I fictionalise that fictionalisation?

We didn't really get a lot done in those sessions. They had all the status and semblance of a dull and dry religious event. We were permitted to absolve ourselves for our sins of the week: the self-harming, the drug-taking (not me) and other self-destructive behaviours. A lot of the time we'd end up smoking cannabis on the hospital grounds. Even though it was forbidden to have outside contact with members of the group, We All Did It. Worth waiting two years for, eh?

Trigger Warning: skip a page, dears, if you're currently dealing with self-harm issues.

It was pretty useless though, because the last time I self-harmed badly, I raised the subject in the group, and Flav completely missed it! It was shocking. I'd taken to using one of those craft blades you use for cutting through balsa wood or something, and I'd been running it along my forearms quite merrily, when I glided through a fleshy bit of the arm. It cut so deep, it ripped a deep gash! In my shock, I immediately put a compeed on it and then tried to forget about it. I examined the deep… well it was more than a cut, it was a wound. It was so deep that it made me feel nauseous. There were squiggly white bits in it which I took to be infection and tried to pick out.

It didn't seem to be healing so I had to go to the doctors. My dear G.P., Ken Branagh, (that's who has to play him in the film) commented, 'You seem to have performed an elliptical on yourself'. He explained that this was an operation which cuts through all the layers of the skin. He also said that the white squiggly stuff was flesh that was growing, and was healing. He did say it should've been stitched, but that I'd left it far too long, and it would now heal into a nasty scar.

I haven't had a prolonged spate of self-harm since that date. It was a bit of a wake-up call for me. All traumas in my life tend to lead to some great spur or realisation. I kept this from my family because I really didn't want to worry them. It was my problem and I would have to deal with it!

In my passivity, another development occurred - this time on Thingbox. This Parasite I alluded to, going under the guise of KittyKat or something (for he loved cats), kept commenting on my pictures, saying how hot I was. And, as you know, Simon's passivity + attention = a protracted and unnecessary relationship. Yes, I didn't see the signs, so I repeated the pattern. An awful thought that kept repeating in my head was, 'I am destined to be miserable anyway, so I might as well go along with it,' a mantra I continued to repeat until a few years ago I am sad to say. I was finding it unbelievably nerve wracking to meet or even talk to people off the internet, not because they might be a serial killer or worse, a Tory, but because I was worried they'd hate me.

Parasite rang me a lot, pissed, and reading passages from Stephen Fry's *The Liar*. He wanted to meet me when he visited London from Birmingham (where he had recently placed his beanie-hat). I had the attitude then that I should never turned down an invitation.

I met him in Soho Square along with his friend. I was sitting on Kirsty MacColl's bench, as I often do when I'm there. We hugged and he said, 'Hey dude,' and gave me all his indie blather. We spent the afternoon together chatting. I was in raconteur mode, as I usually am when I meet new people. It's a faux confidence thing where I become world-weary, all-knowing and oracle dangling. It's a good defensive position. But then I melt away to a blithering idiot when compliments are reared. I had yet to learn that arch-manipulators have barrels of compliments in their arsenal.

We walked round Hyde Park chatting endlessly. He kept going on about how beautiful I was and how he didn't stand a chance with a boy like me. We ended up snogging under a big tree, and I accidentally caught a glimpse of his little boner. More snogging happened in Trash Palace (a now closed Indie gay bar). We left with a promise that we would meet up again.

He was interesting, he was polite, he was charming, he could hold a good conversation… I am trying to think of rational reasons why I'd entertain having such a relationship with a guy I now refer to as Parasite. I guess his flaws outweighed his good points by a massive majority. I would like to say that the realisation was a long time coming, but still within a few weeks of knowing him he visited me, we had sex, and when I say sex it wasn't your full on stuff, it was all rather modest and nice.

We were rampant in that honeymoon period. Despite the fact that I had to go all the way to Birmingham (which turned out to be more of a post-apocolyptic nightmare than Crystal Palace). I do share J.G.Ballard's fear of the overpass. There is something very sinister about all that concrete piled up on top of itself. Before we'd exchanged bodily fluids, I asked Parasite if he had been tested for everything, as I didn't want my unmedicated anxiety taking another battering. He told me he'd had a full STI M.O.T. and that all was good. I took his word for it.

About a month in, he was chatting, and casually in conversation (this was a trademark of his) he dropped in that he'd slept with his old boss, who was HIV positive.

I went into panic mode. I wasn't very well-educated at that point, but still he'd slept with this guy after he'd taken that test and actually after he'd met me for the first time! I was shocked that he had kept this from me. I felt cheated and upset and also anxious for my own health. He reassured me that the chances of transmission were negligible, which if I'd done a bit of research I'd have known they were, but still it was the gaul or the sheer selfishness of him that bowled me over.

I immediately felt inadequate, as nearly everyone he'd mention turned out to have slept with him at some point. He'd describe a sexual detail about them 'he came so much' or 'he was amazing' and so on. This would run into hundreds of men, including best friends, (male, female, trans, intersex, animal, vegetable, mineral) - anyone and everyone! It all made me feel like I was nothing special, that he could still talk about these people with such reverence, but also that he could compliment and describe a multitude of people as 'sexy', whether he saw them in the street or on television. He'd also talk to other guys online, and I'd often find pictures of their dicks on his phone. I put up with it. *Why* did I put up with it? A little bit of me, and this is sick actually, actually liked going out with someone who was so much more of a fuck-up than me, someone I could argue and lord it over and feel superior to, even though he would make me feel miserable. Although I castigated him verbally he still got to do anything he wanted. It wasn't a good relationship even from the outset.

At this point the relationship was a long distance one, so most of it was conducted by phone. I more or less got on with my own life. Another thing about him that was a worry was that he'd drink a lot. Bottles and bottles of the stuff. He told me how he used to take many drugs when he was younger. 'I've tried everything except heroin,' he would say, proudly. At the core of such damaged people, there is sometimes a nucleus that is the cause. Parasite had one that made me soften a little toward his negligent and selfish behaviour. He'd had a terrible childhood, one worthy of a book in its own right. Nevertheless, it's not for me to say what happened; he just told me a lot about it, and it was harrowing.

For a teenager who had problems himself to try and

take care of the unresolved issues of a man pushing thirty was a lot to take, but most of the time I did try to help him and get him on the straight and narrow. And they weren't all terrible times. We had plenty of fun. He got me into *Doctor Who*, which is a positive by-product by anyone's standards. He could be incredibly affectionate when he wanted to be.

I still cringe to think that when I visited him in Birmingham (in this rather unpleasant flatshare) I used to scream the flat down when we had sex, even though his room was next to the living room and people were always sitting in there. And I mean *always*. There was a nice hippy guy who lived with them that always nice to me, and a creepy guy who lived in the attic, and who they all thought was responsible for pissing on the floor by the toilets. Although the whole pissing on the toilet floor saga had a nasty consequence for me. The big beefy bloke who lived there had a go at me, shouting, in his paranoid drugged state, 'It's back and you're back!' which I knew not to be the case, as I always sat down to pee there. It was a place where piss splashing was on high-alert.

* * *

For some reason never made clear at the time or since, I was put on a new type of anti-depressant that had an anti-anxiety and anti-OCD component. They were 'tricyclic' or something. My mood and ability to do things improved immeasurably. I was in such high-spirits, and I felt that I'd lost so much time having spent years doing very little in my depressed state. I could now zoom ahead with what I wanted to accomplish.

My first task was to move out of my parents' home,

which at nineteen, with no job prospects, was quite a tall order. I went down to the local council and asked to be put on the housing list. Due to my long history of Mental Health problems exacerbated by living at home (note: this is only partly true, my parents for the most part, and way beyond the call of duty, helped and supported me through my various ailments), I was put quite high on the list. This was also helped by people from Gay Youth Groups, which was brilliant, as Merton Council had probably never seen such an immaculately turned out bear-waving bureaucratic hoopla in their face. They also needed evidence of the bad home situation, which required everyone to be on their worst behaviour. My family are so sweet. They all chipped in to be as awful as they could be when we were visited, with a guest appearance from my aunt coming over to seal the deal as an agitated by-stander - 'I can't allow this to go on any longer, council representative. Give this boy a home!' She said this as she fainted to the floor.

Joking aside, I was still miserable at home, and these were the lengths we all had to go to so I could be given a place of my own. And I finally was, with the state footing the bill.

I was told I could choose a place to live based on what was in my catchment area. The first place I looked at was a gorgeous granny-flat in Mitcham, which was adorable, but I lost out to a pregnant couple; well, a pregnant woman with a boyfriend. I don't know if he was pregnant too. The second was just awful, but the third was… well, awful as well. I could've held out for somewhere really, really nice, but stupidly in my passivity, I brought the Parasite along with me, to look at this place in Pollards Hill. It was on an estate that looked like a Soviet tenement block. It was desperate. He saw it for about a second and went, 'Yeah, sure, it's fine.' So I signed off on it. I don't think my family were that impressed when they saw it. But I was in such a dandified mode that I was happy to lay my fedora hat anywhere. Yes I was wearing a fedora hat. It was too small for my head so I looked more like a beardless Rabbi. I also wore a cravat, waistcoat, velvet jacket and trousers and two-toned brogues. I think I even had a cane! I quite like picturing that, me dressed as an Beau Brummell, twirling a cane down Streatham High Street, doffing my cap to the local Ghanaians.

I didn't object too much to the place. My parents, such sweethearts, decked out the flat with a sofa, fridge and telly. They paid for a cooker and a washing machine. They were amazing. My mum wanted to decorate, but I never really let her. She managed to get one piece of wallpaper up the entire time I was there. My heart aches at all the awful things I've said to my parents in the face of their kindnesses. It's humbling to think that they really did and do care so much for me, and yet in day to day life you don't see it. If you take a moment to look back… Wow, what amazing people! I know for a fact I wanted to be fiercely independent too, which was a bit silly, as all I did for this was to say, 'I want to be independent, I'm going to be independent,' a lot, without actually taking any action to make it happen.

At first I spent a month or two in the flat on my own. It was spooky at night being there, alone, but my existential panic attacks completely subsided. I'd go over to my parents most days and enjoyed spending time with them more now I had my own space.

The next thing on my 'I Can Achieve Anything' list was to go to college. I was a tad terrified about this, because I had begun to attempt it in previous years, unsuccessfully.

Going to my old stomping grounds like Merton College to try for a Drama B.Tec was a bit of a mission. The irony was that Abigail, a Drapers girl that had also been on Aquarius just after me, was doing the same audition day with me there. We did improv with all these others. I was 19, nearly 20, and the rest were all 16 and 17. When it got to the interview, they praised me on my skill but were all sniffy and said things like 'Don't you feel you're a little too old for this course?'

Another interview for which I'd prepared Alan Bennett's *A Chip In The Sugar* (something I can still remember) as my piece I never got to do, because the guy interviewing me said, 'I think you're too good for this College.' I had to agree with him though because two (and I hate the term Chav, but... yeah) girls were asking questions about my sexuality before the interview, and then went on about some boy who they knew, who was gay, and how wrong it was and how he said he was eating a potato and it tasted of cum. Strange girls.

When I picked up the reins again to look for a college, I found out that there were these things called 'Access to HE Courses', a one year course that could lead straight onto a University Degree. I had only heard of Access Courses being related to prisoners in education, but it seemed that the free man was now allowed to partake. I was giddy with excitement at the chance as I'd always wanted to go to Uni.

I applied for a Drama course at South Thames College and aced the interview. They wanted me to come to a follow up physical session, for which I turned up fifteen minutes late. They had already started in their theatre-blacks and I was too shy to go in. So instead I enrolled on the Media Studies course, led by the brilliant Karol, a wonderful woman, who really put the E into Education (that makes her sound like she gave us drugs, which she didn't - I just mean she was good at her job). I started that September, my first taste of 'mainstream' education in four years. Luckily there were people of all ages on the access course. Single mums, Northeners, alcoholic Russians, bodybuilding Frenchmen, tarty toffs and the like.

I loved the course and threw myself into it. I loved the excuse to be creative and thrilled to all the deadlines, the sub-editing, radio-feature making, filming and doing presentations. It was wondrous. It made me really, really happy. I didn't make particularly close friends with anyone, but was friendly with most of them. We all got on pretty well. The subject of my sexuality came up once or twice. The first time it did, I told people that I was 'bisexual', to which there was absolutely no reaction. I could've told them I was gay and there wouldn't have been an outcry. I saw there were quite a few out guys around College, but there was no-one I had the guts to speak to.

Back at home, Parasite had decided to move in, or I had said he could. Worrying that I can't remember which. My dad had to drive all the way up to Birmingham to collect all his things and drive them down to the flat. Parasite had already made local friends via Thingbox, including a slutty Poet coke addict who had once fingered the racist goth girl from Chapter 5. Nice. I was too busy with my course to worry about him and his proclivities. He got a job at the fancy-dress shop, and he pissed his money up the wall by getting pissed.

In the grand style of my refusing to waste any aspect of my life, my paranoia about Parasite (sometimes justified, sometimes not) was channelled furiously into my work. In the first term of the College course we had to make our UCAS applications to decide which Unis we wanted to go to. I picked

Exeter College to do English and Drama, I think Manchester was another one, and the third was Bournemouth University to do Screenwriting For Film and Television. The reason for the last one was the fact that I had a developingly massive obsession with the television playwright Dennis Potter, and I thought that if I went there then I could be as good as him. Karol tried to steer me away from Bournemouth, saying I'd be a lot more happy at Exeter.

My favourite project at College was the radio feature. Where others made documentaries about Female Genital Mutilation and the local fish and chip shop, I made a mockumentary about a country and western singer called Mimi Laburnum (an edited version is on YouTube if you want to hear it) and her absurd career. I got Rosanne to play Mimi, putting the lyrics to music with her out of tune guitar. Ed played a few roles in it as I remembered he was great at accents. Even Parasite played a small role in it too. It was a lot of fun, and I was, not unpredictably, utterly outrageous. There were jokes and routines in there that were absolutely foul, and no-one batted an eyelid, I was utterly incorrigible.

Another thing we were tasked to do was make a short film. I adapted a fifteen line short story by Franz Kafka entitled 'Just Give Up' for mine. I really went to town on that. I filmed graveyards and stripped our entire bedroom and turned it into a weird German Expressionist nightmare. The Parasite had to jump about naked, and we took hundreds of photographs around Wimbledon. I was hoping to achieve a *La Jetée* type effect with it. Consequently I completely fucked up the editing process and the final effort was crap. It still got a distinction! This was more a comment on how bad the other films were, to be honest, or that the filmmaking teacher liked me. Take your pick!

It was around this time that I was starting to have second thoughts about Parasite. He'd become morose, and even though he had a full-time job, he never had any money and was always taking my benefit money for his fags and booze. He'd given up complimenting me and was never interested in having sex. He didn't even bother to come with me to see the prospective Universities I'd be going to, or to any of the presentation days at College. Those assignments were taken up by my real friends.

Rosanne came with me to Bournemouth that first time. It was the first University I'd ever seen, and consequently I decided to go there. There was nothing that they said on the open day that swayed me. I just had this 'do it' attitude, where I'd be immediately decisive with the first option. It was a good day because I remember when I came home (to my parents instead of the flat for some reason) it was the reveal of Derek Jacobi as The Master on *Doctor Who* which made me very happy. I can often track where I was, how I felt and what I did to the transmission schedule of the revived series of *Doctor Who*. It's my Priest Madeleine!

I felt über-confident at this point. I was in a kind of ascension. I was also getting more and more tired of Parasite and his self-destructive antics. I kept asking friends for advice and help. They all said, 'Kick him out!' which I couldn't bring myself to do. I was on the brink of doing it once, where in typical biopic style, his grandfather had just died, so instead I accompanied him to Norwich and the funeral. He stayed with old friends and decided to get drugfucked to which I responded by screaming and crying in the bathroom.

I was fed up with him and his antics, so I decided to

have some fun myself. I had refined my dandy look into that of an indie-boy. My hair was the longest it had ever been in my life. I wore blazers with badges, drain-pipe jeans and converse, ooh I'd've fucked myself if I could have. I'd always wanted to have fun with a black guy.[28] Something else I'd not got round to at that point. Luckily I found one in Brixton. A charming Nigerian who went by the deliciously onomatopoeic name of Wana. He was an architectural designer with a strange laugh and a blocked nose. We had a nice time, and I liked being wooed. We only really masturbated beside one another. It wasn't even that much but still it was rather enjoyable. I saw him once more but it all went tits up when he saw the scars on my arms, and it turned him off. Shame, I never got my black boy. I mean he was there arse up in the air, face buried in the pillow. Then... gone. In retaliation I went to Argos to buy some coat hanger racks.

During my relationship with Parasite, I was still hankering after attention from other men, people in my past, missed opportunities... all that crap! You remember Pear Guy in Chapter 4? For some stupid reason I had convinced myself I was in love with him, when really it was just a dull obsession. Luckily with the invention of Facebook, one can stalk whomsoever one wants, so after the previous botched attempt at getting in touch with him (I walked to his house in 2004 and hand-posted a letter to the door I remembered was his... It may not have been...) I managed to ensnare him again. This is a great illustration of how ludicrous relationships

---

28 Again, for the over-zealous types, I am jesting. I find many men attractive. Their skin colour is just one of many beautiful attributes. Let's just get on with this and be sensible y'all.

can be when you have BPD.[29] This was what kept me going.

During this period his code name was Dick Clark. Go figure.

16/10/2007, time not specified

Hello A.,
try... try and cast your mind back, years and years, well about 4 years, to the dim, distant past of 2003... when we went to school together? Remember, Simon, the 'gay' one? Erm... yes... who suddenly disappeared, never saw you again? Well... you might not, but I remember us being friends, once upon a time... This is just a nice friendly wave, to say I am not dead... hope you are okay. Be nice to hear from you, toodle pip.

17/10/2007, 21:57

After a while searching the deep recesses of my memory a flash came to me. why yes... Simon... i do remember you. but that was a long time ago... times change... and that's kinda in the past. How time flies, right? But hope ur good. glad to hear ur not dead!

17/10/2007, 22:53

Lovely to hear from you,
Yes, very perceptive, that was 'a long time ago'. All in the past... But I was just a little curious to see how my ol' school

[29] Yeah, when are you getting to that?

chum was doing, and indeed what he has been doing over all this time. Y'know, obviously I'll have to wait for the biography to come out, but if you could fill me in a little... ooh er... (cough) Just wondered is all... You seem happy, and sorted, nice to know life is working out for you.

23/10/2007, 19:16

It's going well thanks! i'm pretty much the same... i think. i'm a lot more confident though...maybe not as shy as i used to be. i remember u used to make me laugh so much.
Brighton is so-oooh cool i was actually surprised that i didn't see more gays, there wasn't that many really, not that im bovvered! there was loadsa lesbians though. haha, the guy at reception at our hotel was chatting me up at one point, was well funny.
Glad its worked out 4 ya.

Note above just how he raises the gay stuff. The penny didn't drop then. I'll skip a lot of the blather in this communication. I'll skip dozens of missives, but the spark that kept this little one-sided romance going was a moment back at school when I was talking to Ash outside the English classroom one afternoon.

I was being my usual cryptic self, all intense, and then I said to him, 'I've got something to tell you, Ashley.' He immediately came back with uncharacteristic confidence and self-control, 'Go on, you can tell me. I won't judge you.' Then something interrupted us. I feel this could've been the moment when I told him I wanted him and he would have been anxious to reciprocate. The reality was quite different. At the time I really fancied this other guy, Darren, who was both incredibly beautiful and stupid, with an even more stupid monotone voice, but eyes as black as minstrels (the confectionery; this isn't some pseudo-racist reference to the Black and White Minstrel show), a perfect toned body and the most gorgeous smile. That's what I wanted to tell him. Why, I have no idea, but I did.

So after all this waffle I was becoming a bit disinterested. I wanted to meet him again, and he was making it obvious in his own passive aggressive way that he wanted no such thing. But we strung each other along for a little longer.
What eventually really got my dander going was the following admission. Oh my word, it was over a year of talking before we got to this point! (he's in italics, by the way, if you haven't got that by this point)

17/08/2008, 23:06

heloooooooo, and good tidings of joy i bring
lol, u shod defo take up the wig hobby, ive enjoyed many a good hour wiv my amy winehouse wig. i luv that crazy bitch.
im glad u sent me a message i really genuinly enjoy reading them.
i think your rigt about not actually seeing me in the flesh again. its not that i dont want to, its more that i wouldn't be able to bridge the huge time gap. but that defo does not mean that i dont want to still keep in contact with you. like i said reading ur emails is great and i get little flashbacks of the old days, hehe. dont say 'it was nice knowing you'!!! it sounds like I'm dead! u

still know me, just in a different format to before!
im glad i was important to ya. u was a good friend aswell. i wish more people wod hav realised you as a person and not been so prejudice.
but hey ho, thats humans for ya, innit?
anywayzzz
i hope everything is goin good for you atm. hows the comedy and all that jazz? i cant wait for my 100 cheryl's lol, but to end this note on a bombshell....i wodnt do much with cheryle apart from admire how amazin she looks, cos well....

I'm gay.

Did u see that one coming? i'd be interested to see if you did.
I await your next message in great anticipation
speak soon chum bag

This was obviously seismic for me, and I entertained the thought that there could be an opportunity to catch up where we'd left off, even thought we had left off with him being entirely disinterested in me other than in the fact that I could him laugh.

18/08/2008, 01:30

Whaaaaaaaaaaaaaaaa!!!!! jaw drops to the floor... no, no I did not see that one coming... at all... unless you are pulling my leg... are you... are you pulling my leg... as usual this is totally unexpected... and puts everything in a weird perspective - the past I mean... although I always had a sneaking suspicion when you said one thing to me... but anyway...

...and yes, I sigh at the thought of not seeing you, although it would be like meeting a totally different person. Anyway, I'd never meet my A. again, because that was a million light years away. Sad, rather sad, but y'know let's never say never because life's too short and all that, (oh dear, Simon's deluded) and bridges don't need to be gapped. People still lose touch and find each other after decades, and it's really weird, sometimes they don't click again, sometimes they do... I know it's a bit odd thinking of a meeting because, well, I am a shy, nervous type, and I know you were shy too... I wonder if you still are... Anywayzzzz I find it really sweet that you genuinely enjoy reading them (words are my craft, after all) and that you get flashbacks. I try not to think of those days too much because they are still a bit... painful, bit shaky writing this, tut, wo'ist me, where was I, back to the land of dreams...

Yes, I have someone at the Party-Store in Clapham who could get all manner of wigs for me, I must get a Pete Doherty one, although I suppose I'd have to leave it in a bin full of piss and heroin for a week... Charming, the thought of such an odious thing crowning me little old bonce. So apart from Wig-fun and botany type fun what else are you up to these days....tell me what's going on on your planet?
I hope your anticipation does not subside juuust yet, and I am now eagerly anticipating your response,
your affectionate chumbag
s i m o n the talking helicopter

18/08/2008, 20:48

I'm not joking. I hope it doesn't tarnish your memories of old.
to be fair i wasnt really sure back then. it was just a niggling
background thought that I learnt to block out.
so i wasnt really hiding anything, its just i didnt know what it
was all about
i wanna know what 'the one thing i said' was though?

awaiting your next use of the english language
take care sonny-jim-bob

end of transmission

19/08/2008, 16:28

No, nothing is tarnished,[30] just my fixed notions of the past have been slightly altered… You confident turnip, you! I would say you are very grown-up, own car, own job, own life… You seem very sorted… Well we both went in very different directions in our 'outingness'… Mine was a rather naive brazen attempt at identity that went horribly wrong... and I think you were very sensible to keep your niggles to yourself for that time... if only I had... It would all be completely different now... and 'self-discovery' is never cheesy. It belongs at the delicatessen counter for one thing. The irony is, I've been out for nearly seven years and I still don't know what it is about. Not into

---

30 A complete lie, heart fucking broken in a whole other way! Again!

the scene at all, can't dance, and cant be vacant... Wo'ist me!
Oooh, that one thing you said... do you really want to know? Actually it could all be perfectly innocent and maybe I read too much into it, so this will embarrass me more... but I don't care... I said, one post-english lesson, 'Oooh, I've got something to tell you,' and you said, 'Oh, you can tell me anything, I wouldn't judge you,' or something to that effect, but you had an odd smirk on your face... Who knows what either of us were getting at.

And I must say I am very happy that you are happy with yourself. 'And you have also assailed to the very pinnacle of your beauty', likin' the indieboi look. I always secretly knew it would suit... Eek! hope I haven't attached a maligned label to your fashionistic bonce. Don't want to pigeon-hole ya or anyfing... I am trying to give a compliment... and look how it comes out.

Well I am glate you are happy, and hath amused you, and I hope to be your verbal amusement for as long as you like.

Looking forward to your next monograph on the way of all wigs

s i m o n the artist, formally known as prick

23/08/2008, 22:47

elooo there
elo matey moo
sorry for the delayed messssage. i did write one pretty much instantly afer readin yours, but then my comp froze and i was jus like 'noooooooooooooooooo'
twas such a long one aswell.

welll anywaaaaaaayz.
i forget now what it was i was gunna say. ermmmm....
well one of the things was that, that thing i said was prob just me being me, cos well, i wouldnt judge anyone really. but who knows, i cant remember that moment if im honest :S thats wat old age does to ya, wooops
also thanks for the compliment much appreciated. by the looks of ur profile pic, you look very animated lately! erm i guess i am an indie boy, but im always tryin to be individual, but dont really work, hehehe.
this is actually a really boring message, my other one was so much better
ah well, enjoy it anyway

02/11/2008, 14:21

oh, I don't know why I am messaging you, I have nothing actually to say as it were... and anything I would love to say there is no point in saying anymore... (cryptic once more)... but you are some ethereal form of acquantance heroin, horrifically addictive and eventually fatal
Heh heh... you'll receive an overtly long e-mail soon, with lots of unusual questions... oh, well... I am sure a mad little thing such as yourself can handle it...

02/11/2008, 16:56

ooooo, you are a cryptic kitty...
tanks for the complimento though

your messages help me grow a few more brain cells wen i read them, hehe
i would try my very best to answer questions u may have
i can handle it!

02/11/2008, 20:06

But I don't know it seems a bit like delving into the past... dare we, dare I... who knows what I might find...

    After this there was an abrupt ceasing of contact. I obviously wanted to tell him that I loved him. Ultimately it took me a year to say nothing at all, and to realise that I'd never have him in any sort of way. What looked so promisingly like a potential reunion on new terms had fizzled out to nothing.

*   *   *

    Such silly impulsive cries for attention from a long forgotten friend was, I feel, my personality scratching at the walls in panic as the first day of my University education was drawing near.

    That last summer before Uni was an odd one. On the one hand I was really nervous that my routine was being disturbed, especially the fact that I wouldn't be seeing my mum nearly everyday. I even saw a THT counsellor about this, a great woman called Katherine, who is the only woman I have ever told all my deepest, darkest secrets to... and in the process realised they weren't that deep or dark at all!

We had a big College send off dinner at a chinese where we all got horrendously drunk. I remember vomiting my guts up at home for ages.

As Uni trundled towards me, I was anxious to make more creative stuff so I could go pre-prepared with a body of work, an identity like that of a creative person. I made this little series called 'Mind Fear', where I played a northern woman in a Bhurka, a Queer Activist and other types which were a little outrageous. There was an Alan Bennetty Goth boy as well in there somewhere. I've never watched it back and a friend of mine owns the only copy, I doubt it'll ever see the light of day.

On the practical side of things, Parasite would have to stay on in the flat whilst I was away at Uni so the bills could get paid, which he was all too happy to do. I felt that it would be foolhardy to break up with him if I could keep him on, paying the bills for the flat. Oh foolish foolish me.

The other thing I did before leaving University, was to renounce my mental health. I was purposefully rewriting my narrative. I had got it into my head that my mental health was something I had willed up myself, and could dispel just as easily. I would go to University, a sane, hale and hearty person, with my decade under mental health services at an end.

Nothing then had prepared me for the fact that my University career would be one of the most exciting life-changing things in my life so far, nor that ignoring my mental health would be an incredibly dangerous and reckless thing to do.

10.
SALAD CREAM DAYS

'When I am... completely myself, entirely alone... or during the night when I cannot sleep, it is on such occasions that my ideas flow best and most abundantly. Whence and how these ideas come I know not, nor can I force them.'

Wolfgang Amadeus Mozart

I couldn't stop talking in the car on the way to Uni. Dad drove us down with mum and Parasite. I just blathered and blathered and blathered. We soon found the Halls of Residence. Crowthorne House bore a striking resemblance to the hospital ward, sans wooden bars on the windows. My parents unpacked and left me to it. Parasite and me to it, to be more precise. I met the flatmates: fascists and whores, every single one of them. The first night Parasite and I went to The Old Fire Station, the Uni's club, but it was heaving so I returned home to the Nintendo DS and the difficulties associated with sharing a single bed.

I was anxious about being suddenly placed in this scarily new situation. My anxiety presented itself in bouts of constant frenetic energy, which soon earned me the nickname, 'Crazy Blazer'. I felt like a tightly coiled spring that had burst into the room determined to perform and delight.

Once Parasite had returned to London, I changed my relationship status on facebook. The Big One. I was determined to get a nice Uni boy on the go. I never actually succeeded though, as my confidence in the all things coupling department was now very low. I was also still messed up on the sexuality front and when it came round to explaining the situation to people, I'd go into long convoluted explanations about it, or I would said I was bisexual, neither of which ever fitted the moment.

There was much to be excited about starting Uni. I loved the lectures and meeting my fellow students. These Screenwriters were my kind of people, a disparate group of outcasts, loners and Jersey residents. I remember meeting future co-writer Scott Payne, a rather shy personification of a script king. When he told me he was from Spalding, I developed a shouting mockney spasm of 'Spalding Boy!' yelled at him along the corridors. I also hung around with a white boy with long dreadlocks that nobody else particularly seemed to like, and then I realised I'd fallen into that autism trap again (cf. bath episode with Paul)

The fact that I'd never been around real people for a long time explained why I hadn't realised that teenagers (post sixth form) had their own predominately pack-mentality ways. I took everything at face value and was completely trusting of people's affection. Mistake.

In that first term I found myself a little emotional, and didn't get on with my new flatmates. I'd spend evenings in my room eating pizza or M&Ms and writing assignments or watching YouTube videos.

The day that I had a real upset and was crying and self-harmed (albeit superficially), was the same day that Scott had an awful incident with his onetime flatmates, ending up with him leaving his flat for good. He ran off and then stumbled into a violent encounter where a woman was being punched in the head by a man, and he gallantly intervened. Surreal. I was sitting watching a Human Centipede parody when the phone went.

'I've just left the flat. I've had to go. They've been throwing potatoes at me. Can I come over?'

'Of course.'

'I'll be over in an hour.'

After more than an hour had passed, I called back, and through the crackly receiver, Scott's voice came once more. 'I'm in the back of an ambulance having my lip stitched. I'll be a bit longer'.

'Okay.'

It transpired that after Scott had seen the man attacking the woman he had shouted out to him to stop, whereupon said man came over and gave Scott a drubbing. Scott came to the flat with a black eye and a bust lip, shaken, but very attractive. We sat and chatted about everything that had happened that night. He showed me his College leaving video. We were up chatting until dawn. It was a great moment for me, even though it came about through less than positive circumstances. This was the nature of Uni life, that close-knit community of bumping into anyone or being thrown together. It bucked me up a lot, and made me feel that things would eventually look up. I wrote so to my Mother that week, in the style of Evelyn Waugh (I've never read him).

18/11/08

Dear Mother,

Here, the long-awaited first letter. Yes the procrastination that gunks up my ideas and sentiments of what 'I really want to do' is still in force. I just 'think' a duck's arse inside-out, without actually following through.

It's a testament to my growth and burgeoning maturity that my pre-warning phone-calls when I would tell you, 'Oh, I am going to write you a letter,' haven't resulted in ridiculous allusions to some sort of forcible estrangement, damnation or suicide note. Even though I didn't, years of conditioning instantly created the thought that sending a letter 'bodes ill' - well it obviously doesn't.

Actually, come to think of it, the only letter I ever wrote to you previously was my 'coming out/troubles at school' letter, which I annoyingly destroyed soon after you read it! Oh, the irony that I'm not even sure of my sexuality anymore!

Yes, 'Why the fuck is he sending me a letter?' I hear you cry! Well, several reasons:

a) I love writing letters
b) It's a great way to get your undivided attention
c) your telephone manner leaves a lot to be desired (*joke*) and only works on the presupposition that we are both *compos mentis* at one and the same time (which, knowing us, would be a very rare opportunity, indeed)
d) I try to spend as much time at Uni as possible, which will invariably lead to not as much contact; a shame, but a must, so it's an opportunity to renew our relationship in a different

form (not that we won't have our little jaunts now and again) but I really think that I won't visit the house... That glass of wine we had the other week and the chat we had there was so lovely. I want to cherish moments like that with you more and more, so need them less and less.

Well that's the housekeeping sorted... Oh, by the way, you had better write back to <u>me</u>, otherwise I shall feel very neglected. Of course letter writing can be a private form of catharsis and self-indulgence for both of us. You can regale me with stories of your job and Grandad's sporadic control of his bowels, and I can tell you what's been going on down here at Uni...

The main priority this week has been trying to get my first assignment finished: a '6 minute non-dialogue script' for which, as you may or may not remember, all I had was the opening image, lovingly provided by my house-mate, the one with the bizarre fluctuating falsetto, a character so deliciously odd that Ed says keep a note-book on her, although I've not been spending so much time with the harridans of late, as I can't stand them. I've already re-appropriated that girl as 'Little Miss Fish' (on account of 'fish' being what she calls her vagina) in a scene with her waking up butt-naked covered in sick. After that it didn't seem to go anywhere. I had this other character, an effeminate controlling boyfriend, cleaning her up and doing everything for her... but it had no real plot... though this has never fazed me in my writing before...

JoJo, a lovely girl, bouncy, sociable, loud, but caring... and more importantly on my scriptwriting course, invited some of us over for a little 'cram sesh' and over a vat of wine the idea came to finish the script. We actually finished it in four lines that took 30 seconds to put down, but it was the bohemian occasion I'd been waiting weeks for. Something like five or six solid hours of writing there to take back with me (only over the way, she's in the same block) and it got wonderful reactions, although they thought it was 'sick'. Mark, the Christian, even went so far as to say that I was 'sick'. It was my intention to SHOCK, though.

There is a girl, Fizz, with whom I am quite besotted. She even wanted me to sign her copy when I said she could keep it! Sweet, er… And she was amazed at the fact that I produced Brie and Cornish wafers at the moment of her 'peckishness'. Hope I'm 'in there'…

Now the 'images' assignment is finished, I can get to work on my second draft of 'My Sitcom' which is an exaggerated version of Newsnight Review for students. It's garnered interest, especially from some of the more bohm scriptwriters, like Arron, the class clown and show off (we vie for attention on that one). Luckily we've joined forces otherwise it could've got embarrassing. He also doesn't drink or go out and we have some rapport. Although unpredictable zaniness can be quite unsettling, he is rather sweet. But then after came 'Why do you always look like you're having a poo?' which I won't worry about, though my constipated face has been commented on many times.

Try as I might, I still can't conceal my contempt and general despair at the human condition. I think the Christian Union sniff around for people like me and I take some glee in blowing metaphorical raspberries at them. I am getting quite tired and bored of always having to defend the point.

I hope that my pact with estranging myself from self-pity will last the course. It seems a bit of an irony that sublime pieces of YouTubery now provide the source for verbal manifestations of my innermost workings. Of course it's always someone in my coterie of dead queer self-hating comedians (and this is not just a plug, because I want his book for Christmas, don't forget). Kenneth Williams' philosophy about existence is always on my mind and it gives me hope (deep irony that he killed himself). You'll have to imagine the mad, gyrating, pontificating and switching between cockney and plummy:

'He came up to me and said 'ere 'ere, have you ever fort wot if there's no-one upstairs, no afterlife, that were 'ere 'n' that's it, have ya? Ever fought that it's all a joke, have ya?' To which I replied, 'If life is a joke, let's make it a good one'.'

I like that, and the idea of existence being something we're 'stuck with' and rather than just moaning on about it… 'We'll all be dead soon' is another cleansing adage.

Well, I must away into the night now… well, morning, as it's Dawn's crack.

All my love.

The Newsnight Review Parody became an obsession. This was a real way to make friends, fill my time, and I absolutely loved doing it. This was what coming to Uni was for. I felt I had been missing out on something vital. I also felt a burning desire to Create, no matter what! Luckily others on my scriptwriting course felt the same way, excited at the various resources we now had at our disposal…

I wanted to make a show for our Student TV station,

a comedy, a satire, a sketch-show and a sit-com; perhaps it could be all of them. I hit upon the idea for a mock 'arts review show' like 'Newsnight Review' (as it was then), where the things the characters reviewed would in turn be sketches in and of themselves. I also thought we would follow the characters' lives backstage. Having told everyone about this, both Arron and Mark, with his Northern Irish deadpan accent and wild ideas emerging from his little monkey-like head, came forward straight away, and I tapped out 'the pilot episode' as quickly as I could. The moral of this would appear to be that if you feel something lacking in your social core, write a six part television series and force strangers to be in it against their will, and eventually, through stealth and Stockholm's Syndrome, you will have something resembling a herd of friendships.

I remember the first time we all sat in a Costa in Bournemouth Town Centre, reading through a silly and rude script, Arron got hepped up on caffeine and provided the jittery iterations of his character 'Jimmy Jinx', while some elderly ladies behind us giggled and cooed at our efforts. One of them in particular became aroused at the idea of gay sex, referenced in the script. She called out across the abandoned trays of lattes and mochas, 'Ooh, I love a bit of dirty sausage!' Everyone in the Costa applauded at her octagenarian celebration of balls-to-the-wall meaty homo-eroticism. I can still hear the tone of her dry tuppence. (I feel pretty sure that's how it happened)

One actor, who was to play Helga Vespasian Signus, the flighty and surreal arts student/adulterer, was sadly missing. I don't remember how Hannaj 'Bang' Bendz became involved, only that we found her both talented and hilarious, observing her ability to to pick clean a whole cooked chicken with her bare hands in less than a minute. With the stirrings of a panel show now before us, we sustained our enthusiasm in the face of unrelenting apathy from the rest of the human race.

The filming was undertaken with serendipity, chaos and a sensual improvisation. I struck up a friendship with a fellow 'Scriptie' called Nuria, who had a background in directing and using camera equipment. She was a Portuguese ball of hair with beautiful teeth, who may well have shared my BPD DNA. She told me she'd worked on French programming through her school at which I swooned, before finally springing it on her: 'Would you like to direct this thing I'm making?' She thought about it for a moment before mewing, 'Okay', perhaps not realising how imminent the filming was.

'Okay, then. Come on, we're all waiting next door!' I screeched, and ran off in the direction of the studio.

We would often laugh and joke at the madness of this epiphany. Everything seemed so fresh and so new. We weren't weighed down by workloads and such. Nuria would direct and edit the episodes, asking me for guidance as she did so, to which I'd burble something incomprehensible which she wouldn't follow and we'd then berate each other for getting it wrong. The partnership worked well, and we made six 30 minute episodes together, editing all the time, even when I was visiting her on holiday at her home in Lisbon. I was so excited at how things I wrote down one minute were being shaped on screen the next through edits and sound overlays.

We didn't follow the scripts to the letter. Hannaj always managed to learn most of her lines, whereas I couldn't remember a word even though I'd written them, but we had an excellent prompter in Matthew Reynolds to call them out before we spoke. This was also how I eventually managed to become close to a young Cumbrian man who shall remain nameless on these pages, other than via the hint that he is the love of my life.[31]

After we had shot and edited the first episode, we had a little screening in JoJo Barton's bedroom. A dozen or so of us crammed into the shoebox space, giggling and squealing at our own stupendity. It was a wonderful bonding exercise, coming together to do something we loved doing: acting, writing, filming, directing, not taking ourselves too seriously, not worrying what people thought of us (though bizarrely people often did take against students making arses of themselves in front of a camera), creating this visual scrapbook. It was all done in such a rush, such an improvised, hazy and mad rush!

By the time the first episode was transmitted, it was already easter. I returned to Parasite who in my time away had spent all the money on my debit card and not paid the rent for two months on the flat. I realised I would have to remove him, and the cats, from the abode. The end of our friendship had been on the cards from the moment I'd returned home. A week or two earlier, he'd rung me while he was wandering around the local park, saying he was going to kill himself. He was a mess. He'd spent all my money. I had to come back and look after him, with fifteen pounds to feed us for the week.

Distraught, I went over to my friend Ed's to recount events and we decamped to the champagne and oyster bar in the newly opened Westfield's to discuss how I might tell Parasite that he had to go. We discussed just how I might make it happen.

When the time came for action, I took to my bed for

---

31 It's Ben, obviously!

a whole day, and when I woke, I went into this speech, which made heavy hints of an ending. He said in disbelief, 'Are you breaking up with me?' to which I emphatically replied, 'Yes'. My heart was racing, but I felt suddenly so happy. He cried his eyes out. I wanted to dance around the room. It was over. I was free! I told him he had to sleep on the sofa, too, which was a first. It was amazing. I'd regained control.

He left a day after to stay with 'a friend'. I felt a sadness as he went, but it was only pity for his way of life. I remembered he'd once said, 'Don't end up like everyone else, Simon. Don't let me alienate you, too.' Unfortunately he had.

With the big change on me, I suddenly found myself with an empty fortnight in a very quiet flat. I banged out 150 pages of script in about ten days, chain-smoking, working around the clock. It was such a burst of energy, with a multitude of crazy ideas emerging all over the place. I was informed by the feedback I got, and by reflecting on who I was writing it for. I will always love the idea of making people in my scripts say the oddest, silliest and rudest things, with utter sincerity.

The other thing I had to do was find somewhere for the two house cats that Parasite had procured from one of his 'friends'. The cats hid in the flat behind the curtains and made odd miaowing noises in the night that sounded uncomfortably like children crying. They frightened me. What was even harder was trying to get them into boxes to take them to Battersea Dogs and Cats home. They hissed and tried to scratch out my eyes. In the end I crabbed the blighters with reinforced gloves. I felt sorry for them, but as I told the woman at the counter, my ex-partner had left them in the flat for ages without adequate food and little water. I just hope they were successfully rehoused.

When I returned after easter we set about recording the rest of the series in blocks. We did full studio days where we recorded all the linking material. Then there were days spent travelling to locations, the most successful of these spent piling into Sal Rowberry's car, with Arron in the boot, to do a Lara Croft parody. We all travelled in costume, and even carried a monster made out of a sheet, a child's bucket, and a castle ruin as our backdrop, magical… Well it might have been if not for the group of eight year old children who jeered and shouted at us during the filming.

For the most part we filmed around Bournemouth with no-one bothering us. We filmed dog-walkers for the purposes of 'interviews', threw chocolate pudding in people's faces, boot-polished Mancunians and abducted one another on the beach dressed in outlandish outfits.

The last day's filming was for a conclusion that we didn't actually have in the can. Nuria and I ended as we began with sheer improv. We went out into the dark night air where she chased me amongst cars as I set fire to my clothes (and some I'd borrowed from kind friends) and went mental in my very tiny Calvin Kleins. This was an oblique meta-ending that I still don't understand, other than it was genuinely interpretative of the idea of us, the people who made this, somehow giving up!

It was perfect. It couldn't get better.

We wanted to have an appropriate send off for *Enculturation* (our agreed title), by showing it in the screening room at our Media School. The Union, who I may have portrayed as totalitarian in the series, gave us money to have booze and crisps, as we sat down to watch the last episode, *The Final Solution*.

Despite the love-in feel of the production, I wanted to move on as soon as possible from the project. I would have loved to have filmed a musical with the same characters, and there had been talk of that, but people were becoming bored with it and wanted to do other things. Scott devised a panel-show, and I was a captain of one of the teams. We put on a revue under the title *The Multifarious Spectacle of Surrogate Ideas*. This was my idea for an Alternative Performance Society. I felt I'd reached my peak at Uni, when I descended the stairs of our lecture theatre hall in a tutu and dress-shirt with bow-tie, clasping a dildo in my hand as a microphone and lip-syncing to Patrick MacNee and Honor Blackman's *Kinky Boots*, for the benefit of a dozen or so people, some of whom were our lecturers.

I always felt *Enculturation* to be a testament to my early University career, when I came out of the shadows of illness and a quiet working-class suburb, to a place filled with creative opportunity. To laugh, be silly and dress up with others who shared the same creative bent. It was beautiful! I love the memory of that time. I wouldn't change a second.

I was making friends so easily. I only had to declare a love of *perre et gilles* sailor pornography and crawl on the floor of our Uni bookshop and I would find myself unrooting a buxom East-German with golden hair and rainbow-flecked flares. Patty was her name and we became firm friends that day.

It was a great time. I was so happy. And I thought it would never end.

After Parasite I wanted to be single for the longest time, but bizarrely when I was least expecting it, I began a relationship with a brilliant guy from Uni which endures to this day and is part of so much happiness and support in my life. If I hadn't missed that drama audition I'd never have met him. See, such hypocrisy in my damning of 'everything happens for a reason' tirade. Ben is, and was, and forever will be my man. Dark-haired, with brilliant blue eyes, cheek bones you'd vote SNP for, just about the perfect human specimen, if there ever was one. He is someone whom I hold in such high esteem, something which has only increased as the years have gone by. The fact that I had this brilliant guy by my side meant that I could get through the best and the worst of times. So here's to you Benji, my Ben, ol' Scruff.[32]

Despite this blossoming relationship, however, my second year fell apart spectacularly. My mental health started to deteriorate. I was ignoring my friends, which caused a backlash I wasn't prepared for. When the bullying and conflict started, I just retreated, avoided and ignored it all. Much of this was down to my anxiety and inability to confront people and call out their bullshit.

I was still making a nuisance of myself. As president of the Alternative Performance Society, I wrote some jokes for our minisite on the Uni's website, for which I got into trouble.

I stood up for myself, my first real rebellious stand, and the formation of a stirring anecdote which I will entitle 'Inciting Religious Hatred', and it goes something like this:

---

[32] I had in fact already submitted this manuscript in its e-format when Ben told me that he didn't mind if I included details about him in it. There was some umming and arring as to whether he wanted to be mentioned at all. He is too gorgeous to be included in a 'bastard' book anyway. Perhaps I will have to inflict a romantic tome as a companion piece to this diatribe.

To: simon_jay
Date: Wed, 7 Oct 2009 15:15:40 +0100
Subject: Multifarious Content
Hello Simon, et al

It's very rare that I would have to step in and take action to amend a clubs' website, but unfortunately I had to remove some words from your homepage yesterday regarding 'religious hatred'. Our Student's Union cannot and will not condone this behaviour and content, especially as racism and religious hatred is illegal. Please see our ethical guidelines below which all students are expected to follow when writing and distributing information in association with our Student's Union:

We encourage freedom of speech and opinion of all students, but also have the duty to protect students and eliminate offensive or corruptive material to be inclusive of all and promote equal opportunities. Please keep to the following ethics when writing/sending us your stories for publication.

As said, we wish all students their freedom of speech, but there is a line that has to be drawn when it comes to abusive speech and potential harm or upset to others. University has a more harsh disciplinary procedure than we do and if they found any disrespectful content on public display they could take courses of action. Please read their disciplinary procedures carefully and pay close attention to point 19.1 regarding relations with others in the University community. I have included a copy of the University Rules for your interest.

Kind Regards,

▮▮▮▮

Hello ▮▮▮▮
   I did wonder when this was going to come up. Unfortunately this is a problem for D▮▮ as she left off the disclaimer attached to the 'religious hatred' line which appears in full on the FaceBook group page. Here it is:

'* ▮▮▮ would like us to point out that with Labour's draconian new anti-terror legislation you're not even allowed to use the term 'fundamentalist religious hatred' in the context of a joke about freedom of speech.'

   I thought it amusing that ▮▮▮▮ hadn't read what I'd written properly and had left it in without the disclaimer, as well as the fact that 'the offending article' has been up on the University Website for everyone to see for about six months without any comment being previously made. Let's just look upon it as a mistake on the part of the person who allowed it to be uploaded in the first place. I did not upload any of this material to the site myself, and whilst I understand that you have to remove it, I would like it to be acknowledged that I, and the society, which is an advocate for Amnesty International and pacifism generally, have no interest in stirring up religious hatred, and that if the satirical footnote (disclaimer) in the text had been included, this would have been clear.

Can the relevant authorities please be notified and informed that our society has no truck with illegality. We deal merely with satirising the fact that one can't joke about these matters and therefore showing the real reason Labour created these laws in the first place.

It is interesting to note that this detail has come up now during our serious discussions over other matters. I hope in future that whoever uploads our material to the site proofreads it carefully before publishing it, and secondly that we're not sent e-mails pointing out things we already know and have no part in.

Nice try, though!

Nothing else was heard about this again. I heard that the person who uploaded it was subsequently sent on a computer course. The 'other matters' I referred to in the letter were that our Students' Union, like at so many new universities, wasn't actually there exclusively for the benefit of the students, but was more in the employ of the Uni to advertise Summer Balls, International Courses, and so on. I don't think they could deal with a contrarian like me who just wanted a space for people who were different. I was oddly treated with kindness, but through gritted teeth, and with regular bollockings.

After that autumn term in the second year, my family decided to take a holiday to Florida. I was excited to be abroad on another continent for the first time, especially as we'd get to go on lots of rides. What I hadn't counted on, despite the diazepam for the flights, was the fact that my family on holiday is reminiscent of a particularly depressing Mike Leigh film. Luckily I had my love back home to write to every day at a little internet café opposite our motel.

A message from Orlando 1

Hello my darling beautiful Scruff,

Blimey, since we got the taxi to Heathrow, it's been non-stop! All you need to know travel wise is that I am here, safe and sound, in good ol' Orlando - the flights were okay - and I wasn't a fearful kitty at all (well justa teensy bit). Only 2 panic-attacks; a personal low-score for an international flight, mind you it's my first international flight…

Been up to so much since I've been here and its only been 2 days - everything seems to remind me of you, from reading about the New Hobbit film that's going to be made, to the Medieval Knights show we went to see as soon as we got to the hotel, this consisted of us pretending to be olden folk from days of YOR, eating chicken with our hands, whilst Americans pretended to be 'British' on horses jousting - it was all rather legendary, which I know you like.

And yes… I don't seem to be able to stop talking about you or thinking of you, they've had enough my family. Hehehehehe. I keep thinking of Paris and seeing you again, holding you, your gorgeous northern burr rushing through my head.

I shot a gun at a firing range today I was dead cool and sexy.

Or so I like to think. It was actually horrible. They are so heavy and when you pull the trigger they push you back. The fact that a child not much older than six was shooting a cardboard cut-out of Osama Bin Laden to bits then cheering, made me feel unwell. Guns aren't for me.

I am a bad sleeper at the best of times, so when I lay in the motel camp-bed as my parents and aunt drunkenly snore in the proper beds across from me, I keep thinking. I keep casting my mind back to September 2008 when we first clapped eyes on each other, emerging at the point where we are now, with all those little seeds of our personalities and their eventual intertwiningness... oh we are so meant to be together!

* * *

A message from Orlando 2: The sequential sequestered sequel

My dad is a cunt basically, and he went too far Again - he detailed all this really graphic derogatory homophobic gibberish, after I made a really silly joke that was innocent and the sort of thing I would usually say - he said stuff like 'you're a giver, not a taker' and then said how dangerous it was to be fucked. It was really unpleasant and shocking, and when I didn't react and just told him I was offended, he got more annoyed and angry, and then the last proper thing he said to me was the phrase 'you're too straight, you're too straight'. I just couldn't stop crying for the evening. I've not cried that much probably since, well I don't know when. The only reason I am saying all this is so I don't feel alone, coz my family pretended not to notice and 99% of the time when I just talk he ignores me.... Anyway it's 'forgotten about so we can enjoy the holiday'. Usually I would let it get to me, along with all my family's weird behaviour, my aunt's constant nasty asides and my mum's complete detachment; but I've decided not to.

I am really enjoying myself. Honest! - This internet cafe I am in now is only five minutes away and only five dollars for the day so I can pop in and out between 10am-8pm, but its five hours later where you are so it's later afternoon. It's dark and snowy there and hot and sunny here, spooky. I like it here. It's got freaky Picasso-esque paintings on the wall and funky classical and jazz music playing.

I got so drunk last night, I slightly pissed the bed - how mortifying - I am sure my dad will have something horrible to say about it. Luckily they are now pretty much letting me get on with my own thing, so before long it will be a proper family holiday. One where I don't have to have anything to do with them.

all my love

vaguely hungover s i m o n

* * *

The Madness of King Message from Orlando III

Hello again,

Your yuletide message made my heart sing, Scruff, it truly did and I think it's a must that you keep in the cold darkness to replenish all your icy mystical sexiness - one of your most exciting and enigmatic qualities, I think; you must sit me down and teach me one day - or over several days, months, years, etc.

Oh, the whole 'Dad' thing is pretty much a distant memory now, just a sudden shock. Thought I could maybe rebuild some sort of a relationship and trust with him, but it's unlikely - anyhow - I am now fully taking on the philosophy of a certain missus Julie of that Andrews variety and 'whenever I'm feeling sad, I simply remember my favourite things, and then I don't feel suicidal'.

I must keep a little notebook or a mini scrapbook of lovely things and some anti-anxiety medicine!

I've done lots of exciting things since I last rambled, which involved me going on a crazy massive rollercoaster called The Hulk which was fun - I bet you'd've liked it! We also all went on a ride where you got so soaked you might as well of been swimming, Damned Popeye! Grrr! I tried to run back to the bloody internet cafe to wish you a merry Xmas, but the buggering thing had shut early, daft sneaks, hehehehehehe!

How was the actual Xmas day for you? Mine was a little unconventional. Went on the 3-D Simpsons simulation ride through Krustyland that was taken over by Sideshow Bob - got a bit sick of all the ridingness by afternoon and actually went to the cineflicks on my own, their cinemas are Palaces! Hugerizations! Leather reclining seats! I saw Nine with all those women in, a nice big musical to release my inner gay! That poor little fella ain't been up to much for a while!

Then our Xmas dindins was in the Hard Rock Cafe as I was staring at genuine Madonna conical bra breast thing!

Anyhoodle, our boxing day is a lazy day, even though I want to do wet 'n' wild with all the slides and tunnels - its been overcast - surprising coz its been so hot some days. My facial hair has been bleached blonde - how's that imagery working

out for you?
    Well I am content at the moment which is good.

all my love,

s i m o n

* * *

The message 4

I have just been fretting over in my head, that I don't want to go back to University either, and just had odd thoughts and depressing things too... it will pass I assure you, I've been trying to force mine to go, but You Have Me! I am on the same wavelength, I had a dream that my hand got amputated last night, spooky eh. x

    I feel almost Suicidal about going back to Uni, so I'm just ignoring the fact that it's coming.... we'll work something out together I am sure...

    Even though you feel depressed about Uni I hope you feel better knowing you feel the same way too... The fact you do makes me feel better about feeling bad, if that makes sense - I will be online for another hour if you're up (I doubt it :P) sleepy scruffage - but I'll doubtless be re-reading your message several times - and I'll be online first thing tomorrow, 10am here... which will be 4pm for you - so unless we're doing something I can't get out of, I'll be here x

Love you darling x

Can't wait to see you x

Hang in there for me, and we'll be together soon

s i m o n

*   *   *

Last

This will be the last internetty message you'll get until I am back in the U.K. So I'll make it sweet. The place I go to normally was closed so I had to trek back to the place I went the first time, (come full circle, eh ;))!

Eeek...and a big bravo to your New Year's Resolution, I hope you don't have nasty withdrawal symptoms from lack of chocolate. It's possibly better to wean yourself off rather than a dramatic gauntlet (is it a gauntlet that comes smashing down?) - I don't know what my New Years Resolution could be? I didn't even think this was the proper new year anyway? – Something Pagan? - I have the usual vague thoughts of 'gym' etc.

Be good to have a proper chat with you rather than these messagey back 'n' forths, as lovely as they are, it isn't the same when we're curled up in bed together, in the middle of the night, and we share everything.

I want to ask you a load of questions about what you're doing for New Year's Eve, but I wont be able to see your reply until the 2nd. It's mortifying to note that I wont be there to kiss you at midnight. Will your household be awake at midnight? I hope so :S

I like the idea of being your special precious angel-boy. I still go to sleep thinking about all those moments when we've been together, past and future.

I don't know quite how to sign off, just sitting here in this weird cafe that has one computer in it, looking out of the window at all the cars going past on the wrong side of the road, thinking I'm on the wrong side of the world and thinking with the right side of my brain.

I think whoever said 'absence makes the heart grow fonder' was making a bit of an understatement, I think absence makes the heart grow tumours, I long for England so I can lay my back on it and think of you x

All my love,

your precious angel-boy (flapping his little wings) x

Who says romance is dead?

*   *   *

As the second year droned on, I swapped living above a garage with a mute animator, a mute sportsman and a rat infested bin for a pomme de terre that contained a lesbian who was in the RAF and liberated her room-mate who was Kuwati born and used to write love letters to John Major. Talking of politics, just look at that seamless segué...

It was way back in September of 2009, that I got two tickets to The Victoria Derbyshire Show. A 5 Live programme that does phone-ins and mundane banter. It was for a special edition, live from the LIBDEM party conference (held that year in Bournemouth) and they wanted a cross-section of the population to put questions forward to those boys and girls in yellow; I fitted the student demographic quite snugly.

I didn't really have any genuinely political questions under my belt, up my sleeve, or concealed near any other bit of clothing... I just wanted to be near them, to see if politicians breathed air like the rest us.

I waited for big boy Nick Clegg, back then someone no-one had heard of. This would be the first time I'd get to see him in the flesh. My trip to Prime Minister's Questions earlier in the year had proved fruitless for a 'Clegg Spot' as the balcony seating obscured the far end of the chamber where the Liberals sit (sat, sat, we must get used to that), but I was instead treated to quite a close-up view of Peter Mandleson who's obviously had a bit of work done, and who was sitting opposite me chatting up a Cardinal.

Eventually Nick came in and sat down and I managed to get in my question just before the news. Eye contact. He was all smiles. I said something coquettish like, 'Oh of all the leader's you're the most attractive!' the room erupted with laughter and Mister Clegg blushed, it was all rather amusing. Although I did say 'I can't imagine you as Prime Minister' but in my defence, it was only due to the fact that I couldn't see him with a cigar and fur coat.

After that brief exchange, the rest of the proceedings floundered. We were asked to write what we wanted from our M.P. on a little card beneath our seat and I scrawled something down in my illegible handwriting and thought nothing more of it.

'Someone Who Is Diligent, Hard-Working And A Human Being.'

I got a charming phone-call from Chris from Radio 5Live saying that they'd like me on the radio, this time as a guest on a panel, talking to lots of politicians. This made my exhibitionist glands secrete a wild brown (metaphorical) mucous. It seemed a whimsical 'maybe'. I didn't have any expectations, you can't. Phone-calls from the BBC promising media appearances to the likes of myself are akin to attractive suitors calling you 'a darling', only for you to be jilted at the last minute for a sexier, younger model.

But this time they said yes!

Proof that even a tired used up old whore gets a break once in a while.

I got to College Green by the Palace of Westminster on that May Tuesday in 2010, sleep deprived and full of adrenalin. My only worries were that the rest of the panel might steal my thunder. As it was, they were lovely and I reigned supreme. There was a lot of backroom stuff going on during those two hours, and I shan't name any names but I have plenty on the practises of the BBC, lovely bizarre types they are.

Particular highlights for me on that day were the various opportunities. First to flirt with the well-dressed Caroline Lucas MP, call Quentin Letts 'untrustworthy' and most of all to write odd off-putting notes onto Victoria Derbyshire's cue cards. One note I put under her introduction to the Shadow Housing Minister was, 'he's got a beard like a bumblebee's pubis'.

After all that I got involved with the local council, leafleting and such for the Liberal Democrats. I was even selected to run on the council, but my heart wasn't in it after the coalition so I let it go. That's as far as my political career has gone, thus far. I still harbor dreams of one day being Prime

Minister, and with people like David and Nigel occupying leadership positions for so long, perhaps that isn't such a ridiculous dream. Not that I'd call myself a Liberal Democrat anymore. Clegg ruined the party for me. I've gone back to Labour, where I shall stay unless they get involved in another illegal war. Then it's green (in fact, 'Vote Green when in doubt' seems a noble adage).

By the end of the second year I was really losing my grip. The fact that I had no medication, no therapy and was no longer acknowledging the fact that I had mental health problems was proving very unwise and potentially dangerous. I had no-one to talk to about how bad things had gotten. Luckily the Samaritans were on hand in e-mail form. Knowing someone was on the other side of the e-mail really helped me get through some very difficult days.

From: Simon Jay
To: Jo@samaritans.org
Sent: 8/3/10, 22:07

I thought it would be constructive and positive to write out a letter about how I am feeling, rather than write it to myself, that's what I used to do. I also used to do it partly for some weird egotistical adolescent vanity; something odd went on when I was a teenager. Now I am 22, at Uni and generally things are a lot better than they used to be.

But it's those few little issues. Not little issues, they are quite engulfing really. First there is this almost constant 'being miserable'; I am of a miserable disposition, it's my personality unfortunately, my body language, and my face give me away as 'disingenuous' or moody, and I doubt it is the sultry, brooding Heathcliff type that people find attractive.

Secondly and this is probably the Big One that is actually the nub of this depression. Loneliness, I am lonely! - I feel I do not have any friends; No One Is There For Me. I am desperate and needy But I control those urges a lot. I will not throw myself on people. I came to terms with the fact that most of my Uni Friends were slightly superficial and immature at the beginning of this year. So in an attempt to be 'better' and not be Miserable as I am when I am with a large Group Of People, I avoided it. I didn't put myself in line with those people that annoyed or upset me. I think I need a more intense friendship, one of those all-encompassing ones, I've noticed a pattern that all of my acquaintances at least have One Close Friend They're Always With! I do not have this at all, and it's driving me to distraction, I can't just get one, it happens naturally and it happens over Time. I don't think I can give that much of myself away!

Last night, My Supposed Friend went to this party with his closest friend and a load of 'chums' from Uni, and I left myself out, because I know they are not genuine and I know I would drink and I wasn't up for it. It's not that issue in and of itself, it's minor and silly, I'm not using it as a guilt-trip passive aggressive thing, like I did in the old days, I purposefully replied to his message that told me how lovely a time he'd had with a cute e-mail. It wasn't long as it was as much as I could genuinely manage. But I keep feeling angry and I want to express it somehow... I used to self-harm but haven't done that in years and I am proud that I haven't. I don't want to go back to that but don't want to have a go at people...

I keep planning pre-meditated 'scenes' but they are silly, I was even sending passive aggressive texts for no reason. I feel bad after and worry, but I want to, I need to Express How Alone And Fucked Off I Am, Properly, Without Sounding Whiney Or Annoying Or Miserable Or The Fact That It Doesn't Matter. I want to be able to say that without sounding like a Mad Person in a group of all these people, being all depressive around them. I want them to at least See this is the reason.

So now I feel like he is a traitor. That feeling will pass, but he can have fun with them all. I can't really. I feel like a fraud if I do. I'm 22 but people think I am 30. I don't want to do Dull Things. I want to have fun. I want to have one friend I can count on. That's what everyone has.

I do feel I will do something destructive though. Not Majorly, coz I don't have the power to do anything quite that big. I feel I am expressing myself as well as I can here. I think mostly of The Loneliness Feeling. I have isolated myself on purpose in a way, behaving weirdly. I can't help it when I am in these moods. It is isolation. I wait for calls and texts from people to see if they care, and then react weirdly to them - A Vicious Cycle.

Lots of good things happened today, and good things have happened in my life. I just feel I am a freak and a lonely messed-up person that isn't accounted for. I want to be accounted for on my own terms. I want to be Self-Possessed. I don't know if that's the right terminology but I want to feel like Me, absolute, just to walk about day to day, with a consistent mood, consistent behaviour, and to be in control, not feel like I have to keep an eye on everything.

So, I will go on won't I? Whilst waiting for your reply,

waiting for some direction and guidance, I am going to try and find a friend... but this Finding Something, doesn't lead to any salvation. I have realised that all my individual depressions are just one long depression with the overriding through-line of 'I'm Looking For _____' and then I'll be happy. But it wont actually change because that blank will always have some unattainable word in it.

I keep planning to turn up to my Uni class at 10am Late because my boyf will be there, and I want him to worry. I don't want to cause him any unnecessary worry. I just want him to see that I am independent of him. I want to prove to myself that I am, but I shouldn't make a big song and dance about it, I should just behave normally. I'd rather not sit next to him though, just because 'friends' will be nearby. I remember when I Could choose who I sat next to, but now I don't sit next to anyone.

I've got to put the sheets on the bed but I am procrastinating or just not wanting to do it because I am all spastic and weird and I find it hard to put the sheet on the bed sometimes.

I can't honestly think my way through 'What I Really Want'... The Whole How To Be Happy!

I never really follow advice properly.

It's felt really good venting actually. I feel genuinely a little better. I shall send this off now, and wait for a reply, if that's what happens. I was going to mope and cry in the dark, well try to. But letting out, actually describing how horrible the thought is that I Do Not Have A Friend, by that I mean A Close Friend that I can spend a lot of time with, I was thinking that even if I did, would I really be happy, is it just a shape this Thing takes?

I do think, though, that I am a miserable person, and somehow that means I deserve to be left alone.

*   *   *

Date: Tue, 9 Mar 2010 18:42:58 +0000
From: jo@samaritans.org
Subject: RE:

Hi,

It's really good that you felt better after sending your first E Mail, and I hope that off loading to us is helping you cope with all these different emotions.

You mentioned in your previous E Mail that you wanted 'to be Me' and at the moment, the person you are is not you - can you tell me what you mean by 'you', and how would you like to see yourself?

Whilst you are so 'fucked off with this situation' have you ever felt that you can't cope with life anymore?

I can see that you are feeling a lot of anger at the moment, if you want to express this anger in a safe way, we are here to listen to you.
This was my reply:

How I would like to see myself? Being me? - That's a good question. I think it would be 'self-possessed' - like I said in the first email, to be a consistent human being. Just being me in spite of how I go a bit weird and different exposed to other people, not miserable, not talking rubbish and being awkward.

I won't enter into any discussion about 'not coping with life anymore?' for obvious reasons, but I do feel unhinged at the moment. And Angry!

Yes expressing anger in a safe contained way, is a bit of an oxymoron... I don't know quite what to do, my thoughts in a lecture this morning, was to go hide in a toilet then smash it up. But this is doubtful...

Date: Tue, 9 Mar 2010 20:57:58 +0000
From: jo@samaritans.org
Subject: RE:

Hi,

Glad that you are finding that sharing your thoughts and feelings with us is in some way helping you to deal with things.

In your email you talked of anger. Could you share more of this with us? Are you angry with your self or with something else?

You also mentioned you feel 'unhinged'. Could you tell us a bit more about this?

Please keep in touch while you are going through this.

Jo

And my reply:

I saw my friend this evening and he managed to cheer me up quite a lot and I feel somewhat better at the moment. I will write again if I feel bad.

I don't feel 100 per cent because I do get easily anxious or obsessive. I'll worry about being so abrupt and changing my tune with this. Perhaps I am being a little premature.

I don't know.

Who knows? We'll see.

* * *

Well, I wasn't premature - by the third year I was off the chart. Very miserable a lot of the time and prone to go off the rails and being impulsive and disappearing for days on end. The mood swings were unbearable. I don't know how I kept going. It wasn't good. I managed to concentrate enough to work on my dissertation, but I no longer attended lectures or any social gatherings. Without my partner, I would have been dead.

There were some flashes of magic. We did a radio

drama in a week called The Bell Chimes Midnight[33] which was cool. That made me happy. But as soon as the dissertation was done, I cut and ran from Bournemouth.

I still feel a deep stab of sadness that I didn't go to my graduation. My parents were so proud of me for completing a degree. The first in my family ever to do so. I didn't want to go though because I was so anxious that I'd see the people who had once been my friends there, and I couldn't face that. Of course it doesn't diminish the achievement, but I had wanted to do it for my parents. I sometimes feel like doing a Masters so I can do it again.

Still, my parents have got to see me in outlandish outfits on stage a lot since then, so it kind of worked out in the end…

---

33 This is still googlable. Just type 'The Bell Chimes Midnight' in and Birst Archive, and it'll come up, if you're so inclined.

11.
THEATRE

'This feeling of power to know that 500 people are sitting dead-quiet in the auditorium and are foolish enough to expose their brains to my powers of suggestion. Some revolt! But many will go away with my spores in their gray matter. They will go home pregnant with the seed of my soul, and they will breed my brood.'

August Strindberg

I was now doing the thing I wanted to in the most convoluted and difficult way imaginable. It was important to cut my teeth on all of this in my own confident and yet naïve way. I worked on projects of one kind or another almost continuously from 2010 to the beginning of 2012. My stamina was unbroken.

Now I know we're not all luvvies, and you certainly don't have to be to work in this field. The reason I am telling you all of this is to show that creativity of any kind, no matter how misguided, how amateur, is deeply prescient in preserving a good state of mental health. It was for me, at this time. Even if the idea of a young ne'erdogood pontificating about his theatrical exploits might send you to the vomit bag, steel yourself for a moment, as this is more about trying to keep sane than simple personal theatre.

The first thing I directed was for Multifarious, since

retitled *The Alternative Performance Society*. I had been paired up with a new member, Sophie Petzal, who was a whirlwind and kept everything together. She had mad hair like an unruly brillo pad, with eye bags more elasticated than mine and a pair of gorgeous stacked heeled white boots that screamed, 'Tory!'

We rehearsed for six weeks for one single performance, booking an actual theatre (studio), where we put together a script with eleven different writers. Each worked on a scene, which built up into this extended story, taking the form of an anti-panto, that is the antithesis of a pantomime, although it was more a subversive parody of the genre.

We had a cast of dozens, from Joanna Rose Barton (one of the nicest women in the world) playing *Captain Rat Pirate Hook Fish-Leg* with her assistant Gerald The Badger, played by Matt (my personal Baldrick) who plotted to destroy panto-land, until Willy Do-It an actor (Arron) along with another actor *The Artist formally known as Prince Charming*... Oh God, yes I know it's all unabashed fringe student stuff. But what is shocking is that cliché, which was once rife, is now barren. The post-yuppie generation take all this far too seriously. They're all making plays with spreadsheets, crowdfunding, investments and Lotto money.

Our costumes were Wilko's Kids Koala masks and ripped bin-bags. We spent days adding as many new gags to the show as we could. I was stitched into my geisha outfit (I played Widow Wanky, obviously). I even had to sing. The people that were in it still say it was the best thing we'd done. We would practise every free moment we had. Every day it was like a blank canvas ready to be filled. I had such freedom. Adding element after element. I could just say 'You're not wearing any shoes, Chris, your character had to sell them on the way to the theatre.' I'd gone exquisitely cray cray with power. I'd even cast our media theory lecturer as 'The Good Fairy', with Sophie giving him lines to recite from obscure German poets.

We came together armed with a common aim. The organisation was demanding, but in those days I thought the only way to feel like you were achieving anything was to stretch yourself on stress. I was even prescribed beta-blockers during the making of that play, something I quickly abandoned when I realised that they lowered your heart-rate.

After *Cause Celèbre* was finished (yes, we'd never heard of the Terence Rattigan play then) I was ready to do my own one-man show, without knowing the first thing about how to do one. I contacted the actor David Benson, having seen his one-man show about Kenneth Williams, *Think No Evil Of Us*. It was sweet was that he replied. I thought I could combine him 'mentoring' me and putting on a one-man show as my placement. Where other people at Uni were doing sensible things like getting runners jobs or sucking cock at Curtis Brown, I was just laying a lot of work at my door!

Meeting David was a very positive experience. I remembered him from the time he'd played Noël Coward in *Goodnight Sweetheart* and the underlying gay jokes that had percolated in my ten year old mind. He was kind to me, explaining what he'd learned and how he had learned it through his life and personal experiences.

My first one-man show, however, was a complete mess. I'd called it *How To Put On A One Man Show* and it was a self-referential journey of how I'd put the show together. People were excited by it, but I never really had the ability, it would seem, to script or rehearse it effectively. I'd done all the advertising work, having photos taken of me in a shopping trolley, covered in paint, made up into posters. I'd hired a venue on the *Camden Fringe* at the rather gross *Sheephaven Bay*. I'd done online adverts with a man covered from head to toe in tattoos. Oh the lovely Blue Jigsaw, another friendship emerging out of that strange day's filming. I'd consulted choreographers (Welsh), hired a director (Australian) and rehearsal space (Shoreditch). I'd begun to rehearse it but was so unhappy with it, that it just made me miserable.

I'd recruited to help try and pad out the show, going to the *Poetry Café* in Covent Garden. There I met Sara, a beautiful girl with an inexplicably bold neck scar, who ended up playing the character of Minty, my photographer. It wasn't a happy creative time for me, though. I think doing things on your own isn't actually that much fun. I can't stress the mess that the project was.

What is also shocking is that there is a 51 page monologue still on my hard drive. A rambling semi-coherent lot of nonsense I don't really want to look through, but I guess for you, dear reader, I can quote a little of it, just to show you I did try.

> *Goes to the little side-table and pours himself a drink out of the decanter, like a low-rent Sherlock Holmes.*
>
> **SIMON**: What are the facts? Well, this talk has the title 'How To Put On A One Man Show'. Oh dear, yes, self-referencing. Imagine that this is never going to be performed, and one day it will be quoted in a book called *Bastardography* to add a little pasture to the text.

Coughs from offstage.

One cannot afford to be cryptic it would seem.

Sips tentatively.

Yes, long after I filled in the forms to appear at this venue and got the go ahead, to create this show with this clunky title. I dared to type it into the Google search engine. A momentary flutter in the chest. Luckily, I observed, no such plays had been written with the same title.

Jesus fucking Christ! Reading that again makes me want to scratch my own fingers off their hinges.

The one man show staggered through one and a half performances, neither of them at *The Sheephaven Bay*. The first was a taster session where I just did a lot of bollocks which people seemed to enjoy, yielding a couple of good write-ups. I followed that with a less successful night at *The Battersea Barge*, with Sara now in a nurse's outfit, wheeling me out in a wheelchair, ready to quote aloud random sections of the Qu'ran. But when it came to do the four night run, I just couldn't go through with it. I avoided it.

A letter was hastily written in an internet café in King's Cross to be read out in lieu of an actual performance. Suffice to say I never even performed the letter. The day after I wrote it I tried to get myself committed to a 'Suicidal Feelings Relief Project' in Finsbury Park. I still remember ringing one of the organisers, Zara, in a panic, and her being an utter cunt to me, even though she'd already taken my money. She said, 'If anyone actually bothers to come and see your show, they'll be turned away'. I was so pissed off, I got Ed to ring her back and give her a bollocking. In the writing of this book, I tried to find one of the nice reviews I'd had. I found instead an unpleasant facebook rant about the incident from the organisers. Très professional.

I recall the letter now as an example of how unwell I was. If I could tell myself then to 'not sweat the small stuff' I would.

To The Audience:

I have left it to the duty of the writer to explain to you the reasons, the whys and wherefores of not having the show as advertised this evening. You have to go back to the beginning of this project to understand. The subject was How To Put On A One Man Show – with the intention that it would contain a narrative of 'The Performer's Journey' from beginning to end told in a vaguely amusing fashion.

It seems, though, that as the Journey progressed, the narrative did not go the way The Writer wanted. The author wanted the performer humiliated. To run dry. To not stick with the ideas. The Writer was unable to write down anything he experienced, unable to learn anything he saw or read, unable to take in what was done, who said this or who said that.

As he approached this first performance, the narrative of his own life became more and more incoherent. The writer subsequently forbade the actor to descend into anything as self-pitying, so nothing was written. He now wishes to explain and apologise to the audience as Truthfully As He Can, because he has fulfilled the purpose and the ideology of the show, but those who know him well will understand what he means, and those that don't, he feels pity for.

He understands the trouble you went to, for you all to come here tonight. The journeys you made, and especially the money you paid to see, in effect, 'something you didn't ask to'. Of course he can refund your ticket if you so wish.

The reason he did not cancel in advance and save you the trouble is that the narrative itself was still in limbo. It felt that it could at any moment suddenly turn about. That it might still come together. That some sense would be made of the project, and the narrative would then emerge. That he'd be able to tell you what had happened on this journey.

But unfortunately, this is the truth of the piece. That the writer/performer over-analysed everything. Every action, every meeting, every person, every conversation. Every moment analysed, until he was no longer writing a show that he could rehearse and perform. He was obsessively chronicling his own self-destruction.

And here is the real narrative. It just didn't come together. It didn't work. It failed. The Performer could have chickened out and just left, just stopped, could have avoided you, brushed it off, considering it to be 'one of those things', but instead, this is the theatrical punchline to the whole private joke that has been played.

This is all that the show has been reduced to. A cinder, a speck, a nothing, an embarrassment, something that all you few have had to come all this way to witness.

So this Theatrical Experience must become something other. Something must be salvaged from the wreckage that has been made. You, The Audience, with me shall speak to one another with the awareness that *we are performing*.

That is all I offer.

You have a decision.

I asked for a cab to be put outside to await me, and I can get into that and leave if you like and you can complain to the management, or I can stay and we can talk to one another.

Yours,
The Writer.

*   *   *

This was a genuine reflection of how my mind was at the time. I wasn't on any medication; I wasn't having therapy; no one really knew the extent of my mental health issues, least of all me. So this show about the self manifested itself in this way. After this experience I went off on my own for a couple of weeks, not contacting my parents or my partner, and then I thought, what about doing a play that has nothing to do with the self? Something classical that I could easily get my teeth into. For some reason I got it into my head to do Shakespeare. I wanted to do Hamlet, and perform it, too. It would be a big two-fingers to the previous experience. It was such an important production for me after that utter flop, to get myself right back on the horse.

I'd travelled from semi-deluded narcissist stress-head, to modestly confident am-dram director/performer in the space of one term.

I cast reliable friends and peculiar acquaintances. I chanced my arm on Patch Morley, a boy in a man's body, obsessed with drawing penises. A somewhat reclusive and child-like vulgarian, he was given Horatio and took it gladly.

It gave me the feeling that I was giving him an outlet to some imagined problem, in that secret self-righteous way one does, and then discounts later as ludicrous.

I cast the big Rosencrantz and Guildenstern double-up roles to two Art Institute boys; difficult and defiant little shits. I tried to handle them with my usual underdog pleasantries, but soon realised, like the others, that they took me for a fool.

Nick Carty was our Polonius, as eccentric and mellifluous off-stage as on. He was a constant mystery. He made our brows furrow more than once, with bizarre ideas about costume. 'What about a top-hat and a monocle?' He'd ask with his trademark lisp, out of nowhere.

'As Polonius is quite an old character, we're thinking a grey wig and a cane,' I replied. To which Nick's usually calm exterior tempered and he protested with, 'There is absolutely no way I am going to wear a grey wig, Simon!' with the tone of someone who has been asked to black-up. With faux frustration, I posited that perhaps we could fashion him an old-man's hump from papier-maché or something, to which he, not taking the irony, said quite sincerely 'Of course, that's fine.'

You'd think with a mind this lateral he wouldn't have been up for some hardline political rhetoric, especially defending the views of the controversial former Labour Prime Minister Tony Blair and his association with President George W. Bush during the Iraq War. It still pleases me when washed-out superficial political opinion (liberal, or otherwise) is met with a considered and well-researched argument, even if I don't agree with said argument. During one rehearsal, Matt, my Baldrick, delivered his, 'That awful man, Tony Blair, illegal invasion of Iraq' spiel, to which Nick replied with his over-thorough explanation of the implacability of U.N. charters in relation to Middle-Eastern affairs. It's a lot like when people come up with interesting anti-monarchist statements, rather than the usual 'they're a waste of money' crap. Nick was a boy who really summed up the saying 'Still Waters Run Deep'. My first impression was that he was a dope and a stoner. I recant!

So began a series of unnecessary early rehearsals, where I confronted myself with playing the role of Hamlet (whilst also directing everyone else). For the first fortnight I didn't learn much more than the 'Hyperion to a satyr' speech. I noticed how the attention span of my fellow performers waxed and waned, how they congratulated each other on their T-Shirt purchases, drinking exploits and various crap, which irked me if only for the fact that I could not join in. I genuinely felt for the most part that it was an imposition to get the cast to actually do some work.

I liked the fact that I was with Ben, my darling Scruff, in rehearsals. I was at first apprehensive for his strangeness, for want of a better word, but we became closer for it. He saw me at my most 'me'.

As time went on, the rehearsals became something to endure as I hadn't learnt lines, was self-conscious, and beginning to fantasise in a drama-queenish way – overdosing? Self-harming? Slashed wrists? And as interest in people coming and conversation about it mounted, I felt a developing ambivalence about the production.

I hit a crisis-point. With the realisation that I was odiously self-pitying, lethargic and self-doubting, it was time to end this downer on all and sundry. That, coupled with the idea that I should work on my self-esteem, drew me to the idea that 'to remain optimistic and see it through to the end' is a viable alternative to running away and self-harming.

I committed myself to a rigorous timetable of line-learning and by the end of the fifth week I *was* Hamlet (or as close to Hamlet as anyone can be with absolutely no stage-training). It was the acquisition of a small tight leather coat that finally sealed the deal.

The most important lesson for me was understanding that even when something seems alien or abhorrent, I could still do it, and succeed.

Matt, amongst others, highlighted to me that Joe (one of the Art Institute boys) was a little hissy bitch and loathsome. I was more concerned with Nick adding extra lines to his characterisation of Polonius. His sense of humour was so deadpan, it was almost imperceptible. When we did the 'accidental murder scene' with Hamlet knifing Polonius through the arras, 'dead for a ducket, dead,' Nick complained that he didn't want me to thrust the retractable knife into his chest. I thought this was another one of his strange 'delicate requests', but it actually transpired that he had a huge scar there, because he'd been born with a hole in the heart, and that there was still something up with it. I reeled with apologies.[34]

Another lesson for all budding theatre groups is never to trust middle-aged Am Dram directors who want the same space as yours, when offering to 'help'. THIS is something the company learnt to its cost when Annie Herridge decided to ingratiate herself 'like a witch with gingerbread', coming to

---

34 Nick Carty subsequently went very quiet after the show and I lost contact with him. I was told he had died of complications from stomach surgery in late July 2013. He was 23. He was such a genuine joy to work with, and I had hoped we would work again together. I remember at the after-party on the last night, he pleaded to me to stay for another drink, but I wanted to go home. I never saw him again. For me he'll be my favourite Polonius and speaker of Shakespeare's lines, Especially his peculiar and unique delivery of, 'You speak like a green girl,' and 'What think you of this, hot love on the wing?'

our tech rehearsal of Act One, five days before we went up.

Her 'help' consisted of slating the entire production in front of the assembled cast. I was pissed off that she hadn't given this 'feedback' to us in private. I told her so, something she didn't really take in, evidenced by her response, 'If you're trying to make art, you must heed my word!' As her mouth ran its crap, and the Art Institute boys lapped up her verbal vomit, Scruff stepped in with his fourpence. To this, dear Annie raised her shrill voice. Here Scruff lost it, and said, 'How dare you speak to my boyfriend like that!' A chivalrous response, yet her damning of our show continued until we had to forcibly eject her from the premises. I still can't quite fathom why she had repeatedly requested to come to the rehearsal in the first place. Jealousy? Snobbery? Deep sexual attraction towards me?

Something must be said at this point about The proprietor of our venue. Patch had told me that the kindly art-loving man we had met earlier, might be a druggie, something that suddenly coloured my view, with all the dodgy cheques he had written. He certainly had a large propensity for bullshit, which was little help in rehearsal, and was prone to sudden bursts of violent temper, especially when there was a reasonable request like asking him to clear the stage of dangerous wires before a rehearsal, at which a volley of expletives would be delivered. Obviously the situation was up to me as director to placate.

As venues go, the pub we performed in was an old converted bank that smelled of dirty socks, had a permanently sticky floor and all manner of undesirables flowing through it at all hours. It was hardly an environment conducive to drama. His 'wife' Louise, however, was a sweetheart with a Davina MacCall level of instant rapport and kindness, like a big sister who makes you laugh and slips you a fiver when you least expect it. I liked her.

We didn't have to advertise obsessively. Facebook alone ensured that 35+ came each night. The £2 concessionary ticket price must have helped a lot. A pound per hour of Shakespeare. When was the last time Shakespeare was performed in the creative dearth of central Bournemouth?

Once I was on stage nothing mattered. I gave it my all, or as much as I could. Very hammy and honest, and I Enjoyed Myself! Seeing an actual audience there brought it all together. I thought Scruff excellent as The Ghost of Hamlet's Father, his presence and oration of the Bard's speeches done to perfection, seemingly effortless for him. Chloe Cook's interpretation of Ophelia was so out there. She took my direction to the letter, allowing me to spit at her during our arguments, to suck on a pacifier during her madness, and to scream and throw herself about during her 'malady'.

Having enjoyed the performances, the after-show elation was subdued, but what matter. I mustn't forget the initial stress, difficulty of cast and so on. For all the compliments and kindnesses I stay modest. For an amateur production mounted by a company of mercurial students, it was a worthy set of performances.

On the last night Scruff said, 'There'll have to be a last ever production of Hamlet. What will that be like?' I threw in with, 'Maybe ours is it!'

Have you noticed anything about this chapter yet, by the way?

Shall I elaborate now, or wait until we are nearer the end?

No, it's not that's it's all about Theatre, although it is, I grant you. That'd be moronic.

No, what it is, is that I Didn't Stop.

I'd go from play to play to play, with overlaps. I'd constantly do projects. It took over my life, I was trying to drown everything out, but also I wanted to run myself into the ground to show how hard I was working. I guess it was also to show I wasn't lazy.

Towards the end of Uni, myself and the Matt Baldrick I have been referencing, decided to do a double-bill; a half-hour play each. It was an idea I had had in my head for years about an online conversation between two men being 'dubbed' over the actors in *The Importance of Being Earnest*. When I say 'dubbed', the actors would speak the lines of the online conversation in the register of the dialogue from the play. Matt's part was going to be a retelling of the creation story, but I persuaded him to create a soundtrack so we could get actors to create a physical theatre piece to go alongside it.

We worked hard on the idea and managed to get two nights to do it at *The White Bear Theatre* in Kennington. Michael Kingsbury, the artistic director, wasn't too fazed by the content. He just smiled benevolently like a human version of Eagle from *The Muppets*.

I cast a friend of a guy from the bad old Yoof Group days, a mistake because although he was a great mover, he over-acted horribly. Stephanie Gunner was amazing in the role of Molly in the first half (she did a full-frontal nude scene on stage, emerging from a big pile of rubbish). She was wonderful in the second half, too, as a fucked-up Lady Bracknell. During the rehearsals Dr. Chasuble had to mime giving Molly a gynaecological examination with a claw hammer, but due to

Stephanie's quick changes, she found herself on stage without underwear. Her pleas to the doctor to be careful of her clitoral piercing were quite moving.

Making the show entertaining was stressful, especially as Matt and me weren't mentally in the best place, but the elation after the second performance when we came off our theatrical high was palpable. We walked half the way home skipping and singing in the rain.

What was additionally bizarre was that right after doing that play, I ended up directing a further two plays in succession. We were Edinburgh bound to do a show, whilst I was also working on a play about a black British family in south London coming to terms with the loss of their mother. The project became important to me after the first director (I had only meant to assistant-direct) fucked off after one rehearsal, in which he only used NLP and subsequently wrote e-mails to all the cast saying how awful the production was. It was a community production where Comfort (the writer / producer) had been awarded money to do her show, and her script. I fought back immediately and willed it to go on even though I had no idea about what I was doing. I am happy to say despite numerous walk-outs, financial fuckeries and whatnot, the play finally went up at *The Lost Theatre* to full houses, amidst rapturous applause.

The idea for the Edinburgh show was a review piece talking about all the shows at the Fringe that would then descend into a real drama, and a bit of a Greek tragedy to boot. The problem was, there was no script. My mind was frazzled and we hadn't had the time to write one. In the end we adapted it from the lines of a dossier I'd written. It was a mess, though a lot less of a mess that I had thought it might be. It was called *Culture Bucket* and told the story of a review show led by an evil old matriarch Mariella D'Arkness, her adoring servant Neil Gaye, a simpleton DJ Sam Warbarton (me, in a cute inoffensive role) and Jake something or other, the voice of reason and technician. The 'plot', if you could call it that, centred around Kate Krushnev, a missing panelist on a review show, who had died by suicide. Mariella was Neil's mother (even though he fancied her without realising). It was all supposed to end in a grizzly murder.

Some time after this I was doing a performance at a Christmas party when I bumped into the Head of the National Student Drama Awards (who had come to see the show) and I said, 'Oh you came and saw *Culture Bucket*', and she leaned in and with a wince said, 'Yes, very hard pitch that show. Very hard sell.' Then she leaned back with a smirk on her face, hoping I'd be reduced to a puddle. Instead, I smiled benignly and said, 'Okie dokie.'

Her face dropped visibly. It is the best reaction to ill comment. When van men sometimes shout abuse at me as they drive past, I will always smile and wave at them. Sometimes I even blow them a kiss.

Edinburgh is an experience like no other. I urge every living soul to go at least once during their life. It's an explosion of art and creativity, and it was incredible to be part of it with our humble first show. Of course I was a complete stress-head during the whole thing, but I did it. I did it! It was one of those bucket-list moments.

As soon as I got back, I was already planning my next production. That's the funnest part, thinking about what you're going to do next. The actual doing it is the nightmare.

I wanted to do another Shakespeare, as I had got it into my head that I'd do a different Shakespeare every year. This time I picked *The Tempest* because it is magical and I thought I could cut it up into sections.

I set about casting all the roles. I had a whole day and dozens of actors to choose from. I wore a 'National Theatre of Scotland' tee-shirt that Scruff's dad owned and had given me to psych the actors into thinking I was hot shit! Or is that shit hot? I was warm fecal matter of some kind, in any case. I also had with me Anna, a Latvian set designer I had met off the internet. She was cute, clever and unnervingly beautiful. She terrified me. She helped me cast and I was excited that it would be my seventh play, and the first with an actual set. Set design was important in drama production, apparently.

I was looking for good actors, but also actors who would be good to work with. It wasn't really a professional aim, but I wanted to be able to go on a learning journey with them. I had originally wanted David Hoyle, a unique queer cabaret performer and actor who crops up in everything from Chris Morris's *Nathan Barley* to *Velvet Goldmine* (which starred Christian Bale).

I contacted him about the idea of playing Prospero and he was keen. I even sent the script to his home in Manchester, but when we got down to the dates, he couldn't do it. I received a lovely mobile phone call from him.

'Sorry love. The sound, it's off. It's the signal. I'm leaning out the window here for a bit of it. As much as I'd like to, I can't do the play as I'm attached to another project for the next year now. Sorry.'

Bless him.

I was gutted, though in retrospect how it would

have worked having him in the cast I hadn't actually thought through.

Another element (there were so many) was that I got a friend, Ben Smith, to rewrite the songs in the show, adding musical orchestration to them so they could be played on live guitar.

Where it started to go wrong was that I had my arm twisted in the casting.

By the cast themselves.

My casting days stretched over several sessions with some interesting choices like comedian Gerry Howell as Trinculo, and Yuriria Fanjul as Caliban (who doesn't like a bit of gender-swapping?). I thought they worked well, but I really didn't like Matt, who had put himself forward for Prospero. He was a big brute of a man who wanted to play the part a little too much.

I was also looking at actors who had had experience of Mental Health Problems, which might translate into their character. Matt had begged to be part of the show, but later on I found out he'd bitched about it all, including me. The worst part was the girl who played Ariel. Don't get me wrong, she was a good performer, but she was just shocking as a person. Demanding, rude, controlling, and deeply unpleasant. Really undermining. Other than that she was fine.

My mum often cites the staging of this play as hilarious, and she has a point.

Kevin, who played Antonio, had never had a big part before. He was very much the ham in the role as you might say, bless him. His monotone exclamations of 'Deep in the ooze,' and 'I long to hear the story of your life,' made her chuckle. But the reason he was in it, and I am glad he was, was because he needed the opportunity. He'd also provided me with free rehearsal space for the entire duration, so it seemed unkind not to give him something back.

We rehearsed at the back of an Irish Pub in Streatham Hill. The room had no partition, and the drunks at the front of the pub could see in and could often be heard commenting during the performance.

I had to deal with so much bickering and complaining from the actors, that I felt like I was a human pin cushion.

In the end I hired a flame-haired Australian woman, Tammie, who saved my bacon, having been installed as my assistant director. She was a saint for me.

They were right. I didn't know what I was doing, but I was learning. I was also producing.

There were a few slip-ups, like one of the actors breaking an ankle during rehearsal and having to be replaced at short notice. Ditto the guitarist (not because he broke anything, but because he was shit).

Anna was doing the work of four people, making all the costumes as well as the entire set, which was a red and green chess-board.

By then I was running on empty. Ariel was being a cunt. I had lighting breathing down my back about getting gels. I had to run all over the place for props and get to rehearsal on time. And I just didn't have my heart in it. And for all of it, it wasn't what I'd set out to direct. I'd thrown some things together, but so much had got lost. I remember coming home and just crying my eyes out to my mum, absolutely hating it!

I didn't even go to every performance, I loathed it that much. It got one-star reviews, one notably saying, 'I wished a tempest would sweep away the theatre'.

What was even more galling was the actors (anonymously) had been slagging each other and me off in the comments section below.

I was glad when it was all over and we had painted the theatre set back to its original black.

Matt said, 'Did you get what you wanted out of it?'

I lied and said yes.

The worst part of it all was just how rigid my ideas had been about the project. I hadn't thought I could fire anyone or change things to suit the situation better. I had just lamented and fallen into despair.

Michael turned to me one day during the production, and said, 'Don't get ill over this. It's only theatre.'

12.

SHE WORKS HARD FOR THE MONEY

'You gain strength, courage and confidence by every experience in which you really stop to look fear in the face. You are able to say to yourself, I have lived through this horror. I can take the next thing that comes along. You must do the thing you think you cannot do.'

Eleanor Roosevelt, You Learn by Living

After the experience with *The Tempest* my rigid thinking decided that directing theatre perhaps wasn't for me. I continued writing, this time with Scott (Spalding Boy) from the University on a new one-man show. I found my mind was splitting off into two directions. One side wanted to continue doing creative things, whilst the other more rigid side demanded that I get a job and move out from my parents as soon as possible. It was that bad mantra that you're going to be miserable for the rest of your life anyway, so why bother trying to make it enjoyable? tickling at my better judgement.

This negativity gnawed at my brain, in spite of the outward appearance that things in my life were enjoyable.

I'd been signing on for six months with little hope of a job, eventually moving the Job Seekers' folk to feel they might improve my job prospects with a placement. Funnily enough they were only able to find me a placement at the Job Centre itself. Such strangeness aside, it went quite well, despite the fact that I was treated with contempt wherever I went.

The job was dull because I wasn't really allowed to do anything else other than talk to the staff and customers that came in. I like having conversations though, so it wasn't completely unpalatable.

Sometimes I'd fall asleep when the activities slowed. I got on well with my personal worker person thing (I can't remember the inexplicably moronic titles that we were all given) who always treated me well, as did her rather gay Mengele-looking assistant who hid round the back most of the day. I learnt all the tricks of the trade, such as the fact that the desks were set wide and long to deter the demented unemployed from having easy access to your face. The little pens that failed to write were placed everywhere to demoralise the work-shy and benefit hungry. There were panic buttons strategically positioned under each table.

During one Wednesday morning meeting, there was a laughable role-play set up, where one of the young dishy male staff donned a hoodie and said to the customer service lady behind the desk that he had a knife.

The lady said, 'Can I have the yellow folder?' to her colleague.

'Why did you say that?' she responded.

The group leader said, 'I thought that was the code term to use if you were being threatened with violence.' There were then several different responses from the other staff.

'I thought it was blue', said one.

'I heard red,' said another.

It floundered after that. It seemed that the people who worked at the Job Centre were actually ordinary human beings like the rest of us.

What excited me in addition was that I could now put 'Worked at Her Majesty's Department of Work and Pensions' on my CV.'

For someone who has never had a long spell of employment at the hands of other people, 2012 suddenly had a lot going for it. I managed to get some 'supporting artist' or 'extra' work through local agencies. One was *Jab Tak Hai Jaan,* a Bollywood film, Yash Chopra's last. It was filmed from morning to evening on the South Bank. We were more than just your run of the mill extras, as I was one of the 'buskers', which meant I put on a suit and white make-up, which was touched up by the make-up lady.

'Let me just wipe away a bit of the breakfast,' she said disdainfully, as she removed the lump of hash brown hanging from my gob.

It was interesting to be on an actual film set, though I was useless at learning the Bollywood dance moves. I thought the stand-in for Shah Rukh Khan was the star. He only deigned to turn up once the masses had been educated. It was a long shoot, involving me doing a ridiculous dance and making faces. I don't know if I made the cut or was faded out. During my Chaplinesque dancing routine I caught the attention of this young boy, who couldn't have been more than 12. He had Justin Bieber hair, a pierced diamonte earring, and skinny jeans. He bounded over and as he approached I made a face at him, a ridiculous expression, expecting him to be a vacant reproduction of his vapid generation. In the event he returned the expression with subtlety and introduced himself with a confident camp aplomb. I had originally thought him to be a tom-boyish girl, but he proved a delightful boy: funny, sweet, flamboyant and happy. He effervesced.

Later on, the robot busker mentioned him, saying how 'sure of himself' he was, and how sure he was of his own sexuality. A sudden twang of anxiety fluttered in me, but it didn't seem to register on anyone else's bonce. 'It took me years to work myself out but look how well he's doing,' said Mark/Robot.

It all put a bit of a sting in that day, because I suddenly couldn't stop thinking about that boy being happy. I was so proud of him, this beautiful sweet child, a boy I'd be honoured to call a nephew or son. Happy, camp and perhaps sure that the connotations could mean he is gay and not fazed or even troubled that through the haze of adolescence into adulthood he'll be described, or may even self-describe, as gay. This boy, Jack, I think, was from an acting family where such things may have had more positive encouragement, but I had been the same as Jack; a bright, clever, camp and gay child, but I never identified anything I was or did as Positive, especially my camp, effeminate nature, my crossed legs, swanning about telling stories, being loud, gesturing, acting, skipping, putting on girls' clothes, or wanting a handbag. I was lifted by the idea of Jack. I have never sought to assume anyone's sexual orientation, whether they be twelve or 82, but to bestow praise on a child that's fabulous and loves the fact that he's fabulous, filled my heart with joy. That initial sting of anxiety went when I realised that I could bask in my own fabulousness as a gay child and free *him* from the prejudice that had surrounded him.

I did some other extra work, one being an audience member in a 70s sex club for *The Look of Love* directed by Michael Winterbottom. I sat next to Steve Coogan who was in a particularly grumpy mood, and a rather 'tired' looking Anna Friel, who I initially didn't recognise and thought her another extra. She asked me for an ashtray for her fag, tapping her cigarette ash into it as I was holding it, as if I were expected to carry on holding it indefinitely. I said brusquely, 'Take it then!' which she did, rather impolitely. I only ever liked her in Brookside.

I continued to get calls on my phone for the various projects I had offered myself up for. One had been to be a quizmaster, which was a bit out of the blue. I even went to meet this bearded bloke who talked me through his system at a pub in Finsbury Park. Even weirder was one just round the corner from a friend seeing a new flat, which I escaped to and assisted her with. I love serendipitous moments like that which feel like you're in a sitcom. I only ever did one quiz night with that company, well, one and a half. You got paid £10 for turning up whether the gig went ahead or not. I was so unbelievably nervous with pub crowds and whether the microphones or the sound clips would work, things like that. The only time I did do it was in a nice little pub in Putney, where I forced myself, even without the microphones, and ended up chatting to the quiz teams after. They were a strange and conspiratorial bunch. When I had to do it again, I was so anxious I had to call beardy to cancel, making up some cock and cock story that I had a friend who was in hospital – insane – yes that box of frogs had yet to be sedated.

All this was going on during my prep for the developing one-man show. Details will be squirted between your eyes in a few paragraphs. I just want to mention it as the show was bubbling away in the background during all of this. Added to which I got another phone call, this time from Age UK. Serendipitous, see?

Apparently the course leader Caroline needed someone to teach creative writing as a class. I didn't know how she had got hold of my information or even whether this would be something that I could do, but my mind clicked into gear and whizzed and whirred. I did once have a dim memory in one of my fits of mania that I was going to do freelance creative writing classes and set up an account on the 'school of everything.' That was in 2010, so it only took 2 and a half years to get a response, which was gratifying.

When in doubt as to whether my abilities enabled me to do a particular job, I always said 'yes' and then tried to get out of it later. I really wanted to do well, and got all my prep ready as best I could for this creative writing class of oldies.

On my first day in Twickenham I couldn't find the scheduled venue and ran up and down the street in a right panic. When I finally got to my destination, my one and only pupil was sitting there patiently. Her name was Eileen, a bespectacled lady and a natty dresser too, who had a demeanor and a general down to Earth intelligence that made me place her in her early sixties. She turned out to be 83.

I felt as though I might have let her down because I was all frazzled, and I'd also only planned for a more group-based lesson. I kept asking her for reassurance though in the end I managed to get through and impart some stimulating exercises for writing. Caroline said it would pick up, but it never did, I'd get three or four at most in my classes, which I didn't mind, but they were never the same three or four. Eileen was always loyal and did all the exercises in an exemplary fashion. There was dotty Deedee with her poetry and racist John with his stories about meeting Winston Churchill on the brow of a hill, Maureen the former chemistry teacher and Sheila with her fears of nuclear war and infant mortality. They were a great bunch and I loved talking to them, though I found it hard to steer it into a creative discourse.

My mission statement was that anyone could be creative, with a bit of additional ethos stolen from Christopher Hitchens - If you can talk, you can write - but leaving out the bit where he says 'but how many people can actually talk?'

It was just a case of unblocking the self-doubt. I felt it was a sound thing to do; there was something very exciting about having people who had lived long and fulfilling lives coming to creative writing as a new discipline. Annoyingly a lot of them did have crippling self-doubt: 'Oh I can't do anything like that!' I'd probe why, and stories of either parental neglect or more often educational neglect were recounted.

In a last ditch attempt to get the creative writing class off the ground I gave a talk to the 'debating group'. I waxed lyrical on the importance of being creative. The people who attended it were fascinating. Former actors, politicians, midwives, all with their own spin on things. There were a few rotten eggs in there: 'I thought this was calligraphy,' one woman piped up, and when I asked her what she read, she said 'I don't read books, I buy my Daily Mail and I read that cover to cover,' to which I responded, 'Now I know why you can't read a book.' She didn't come the following week.

* * *

By March, Scott and I had got the draft of a play together called *Is He A Bit Simon Jay?* and set about looking for a director to bring it to life. We wanted the show to be original and have a professional look about it. We decided that it would describe the life of a character *Simon*, who has died, and we would look back on his life through everyone who had played a part in it. As an acting professional I would also need someone to work on my confidence, after having such a bad experience with staging my previous one-man show, and because I genuinely still had little idea about what I was doing. This was the blurb for our show, just in case you want to know what it was about:

Spanning nine decades and dozens of characters, Is He A Bit Simon Jay? tells the story of Simon Reuben Jay (1931-2013) from his death to his birth from the perspectives of the people he met along the way, a tragic tale of a life not lived, as seen by those who were there.

Call it an eccentric whim, but the only person I felt comfortable directing me was an eccentric Mexican actress who specialised in Opera. She also possessed a panache for dressing up as Shakespearian monsters. Yuriria Fanjul was a wonderful, positive force for me. She took a jabbering, self-deprecating boy and turned him into a one-man speech spouting machine… *You should check out her work online.*

Fortunetely we had lots of time to explore and develop the script into performance, with the aid of a basement room in Goodge Street where we rehearsed and developed and developed and cut and chopped and changed and rewrote. The rehearsal period was so much fun. Yuri did amazing warm ups with vocal exercises and thumping my back with her fists really hard. We dined on the finest Tesco sandwiches, and talked of plays past and present. We also came up with voices and movements for characters. I remember so many great scenes which were rehearsed and even sourced for costumes and props; such as a Swedish Mortician 'tidying' up Simon's corpse in the story, only to be scolded for the fact that he already looked horrific. Then there was Simon's daughter on the antiques roadshow, a few extra Linda (Simon's demented mother who was in prison) scenes and all sorts of shifts in the plot as the whole thing gathered momentum.

The plan for the design was to have full-costume changes, props, and a backdrop, all diligently sourced by Yuri and sewed. We did a lot of the prop shopping together. An amusing day in Dalston, Kingsland ensued, trying on wigs designed especially for sexy black women (a group of which I am an honourary member), and polka dotted bras from Matalan.

As the costume 'quick changes' were so difficult, they required a lot of prep, so we employed a stage-hand who very kindly volunteered for us. He was a rather attractive young man called TJ who helped me backstage… TJ… oh TJ… *cough*… anyway…

Time rumbled on, more of the play was cut, and we had people come to see rehearsals including a tutor, Dan (think Robert Mapplethorpe) from La Coq, who was very helpful in discussing the movement and how we could improve upon a set, also asking questions of Simon's character… and central themes of the play, which we wanted to work on answering.

Another thing that was subsequently realised very differently, was the wedding scene where there were about half-a-dozen characters. In this instance we used puppets which I manipulated… all made by Yuri. Another thing she made was the inaugural claw, which was designed to symbolise the character of Simon and how he develops in the story.

Time was now rolling on and things were getting out of hand. We'd had all the costumes made and altered by a professional costumier, all velcroed down the side. We'd booked the *Etcetera Theatre* for two shows in one night and picked out songs for transitions, including a myriad of ideas to indicate that time was going backwards. I recall Scott frantically writing down the years on bits of paper on the morning of the show, so strong was our worry that no-one would get the fact that we were travelling back in time…

Before we did the first two performances at the ETC. we wanted to test whether this potentially overblown and complex performance would actually work…

A tiny little function room above the Distillers Arms in Farringdon proved to be the place where the show was performed for the first time in its entirety in front of other human beings. We had Mischa Resnick (director from the aborted first one-man show), Dan from La Coq and Shem Pennant (funny man who provided one of the most immortal lines in the show 'Oh it's Mr. Tibbles, my daughter's pet hamster, I am psycho-analysing it, it thinks it's a crab') as our audience, as well as Andrea Miller on sound, and TJ back-stage. The show exceeded its desired length by almost 30 minutes. Sometimes it would take up to five minutes to change costumes. Things ripped, and would fall off. I Became Frenetic, although joy of joys, even though that all happened… It Made Sense…

We asked the audience, tremulously, 'So did you get (a), (b) and (c)…' and they replied: 'Yeah, obviously…' which was a boon. Shem also provided the extra gag-injections. The main thing we quickly learned was that we couldn't have full costume changes! So we got rid of the costumes, and just had an item of clothing; but still the wigs, still the props; we still needed TJ!

On the day of the performance, the Scientology-themed funeral programmes were printed and set out on the seats of the theatre. We carried a full size dining table from Tottenham Court Road to Camden on the tube and the stage was set. We ran through twice, before I performed the first show at 2.30. We sold out, the audience was warm and receptive, and they even laughed in the right places, and laughed a lot. It felt great, like it had landed, and there really was now something of potential here.

The second show was slightly more subdued. I was exhausted. It went well, but I felt weird, and afterwards I was chronically out of it. So much so that Yuri fly-tipping the massive table in a Skip in Camden Market didn't seem all that outrageous. Scott and me were happy with it, and began a rewrite based on what we had learned. Yuri was less happy, as she thought she hadn't done the work justice, but we were very pleased with her work, and were gutted when she decided not to continue with the project, as without her, I genuinely doubt I would have ever embarked on such a daunting task.

As that April paved its way into May, I became listless. I was suddenly terrified that I'd spend the rest of my life at home, and that I'd never grow up. I'd given up my own flat all the way back in 2010 as I had never used it, and my poor mum had kept up paying the rent on it for almost a year. Remembering these acts of kindness fills my eyes with tears. What good people. I'd also got it into my head that because my contemporaries had moved out and got jobs and were heading in some sort of direction with their lives, that I should be doing exactly the same. Ever the resourceful chap, I asked

Patty if there was any chance I could do some work experience at the book shop where she worked in Oxfordshire. Luckily there was, and I decamped to Witney, the former blanket making town and David Cameron's constituency (*Hammer horror crack of thunder*).

The intention was to stay for the week for the work experience, so I would be better equipped to get a job in London. Patty was house-sitting for her friend's lovely kittens and the days at the book shop were long and boring. They didn't allow me on the tills, so my main role became that of shelf-stacker and alphabetiser. I also got in on the ground floor of all the gossip, of which there was plenty. It was stifling because the shop was tiny, a real village bookshop. My favourite part of the job (and one the shop prided itself on) was talking to customers about books. I could do that and I knew I was good at it.

It wasn't a great time, though. I was so anxious about getting anything wrong that I felt constantly inadequate and on edge. Anxious to the point where I would physically shake, feel sick and my hair would fall out. Still, I didn't see that there was anything wrong with me.

Having such a close friendship with Patty, someone with a similar mental make-up to me was fun and intense. 'You're Somebody's Mother!' we would scream in each other's face simultaneously, such was our love of poor taste comedies like *Family Guy*. I respected her and felt as sensitive to her issues as she was to mine, but it got messy in the work situation, which was something we hadn't really expected, being such good friends.

Patty worked me hard to bring me up to speed. During the week's work experience, the job of weekend bookseller came up, for which I was interviewed. Patty put me through my paces to make sure she wasn't accused of nepotism, which was ridiculous as she was the one who ultimately got to choose if she wanted me in the job or not. She knew I could do the job, was loyal, and wasn't dirty or gross.

She said I did well in the interview, and intimated that the job was mine. There was then the issue of where I was going to live. Patty, bless her, Saint Patty she should be as she has performed many miracles in her life: two of which the act of turning wine into stomach acid, and not murdering the entire population of an inbred backward-looking township. At my request she found somewhere for me. There was another room going spare in the house in which she lived, under the auspices of her rather quiet and Dennis Nilsen look-alike landlord. Nilsen seemed a rather nice guy, posh and odd and socially awkward. I'd never really had much cause to think about him. He said the room was as good as mine if I wanted it. Mistake.

I toddled off back to London the week before the London Olympic Games were due to start, waiting to hear if I had got the job.

Back home I was already planning what my room in Camerontown would be like and how I'd decorate the space. Then, a phone-call came through: 'I am so sorry, darling, they've said because I interviewed you that you're going to have to do the interview again.' I was numbed. Upset that my dream of a grown up normal life had been shattered before I'd even started dreaming it. I cried my eyes out.

All wasn't lost though and I eventually adopted a 'what will be will be' mode of thinking. Mum and I weighed up the pros and cons of moving out, and actually the cons seemed to be winning. If only I had listened. People were telling me,

'Why do you want to leave London? You're doing so many amazing things here.' Yet my thinking was rigid, along with the usual stubbornness and determination. This niggling voice kept at me, saying 'You've never had a job. You've never tried to be normal.' I also had adopted this apocalyptic line of thinking that the way the economy was going, I wouldn't be able to rely on my parents forever. So I returned to Oxford the next day to have another interview. It went well, and ironically the decision to appoint was left with Patty.

The following week I moved in. I was so excited to have a room of my own. I got it together. I set up my bank transfer with Nilsen, who never looked me in the eye or explained anything properly. The first week there I felt it was going to work out. I felt confident that things were finally going to work out. Mistake.

The first warning sign should have been the behaviour of the landlord. A man who never set any rules, which meant that he could administer his dominion as an ad-hoc Emperor. He decided not to say how unhappy he was at my moving in until everything had been dotted and signed, and then one evening, bedecked in his Chinese dressing gown, he burst out of his room and launched into a volley of abuse, mainly directed at Patty, before slamming the door behind him.

What's going on? What's the meaning of all this? It's not just the noise; it's been like a madhouse these last few days! Doors and windows left open, using the kitchen every day! Up at all hours! And now guests staying over - in my rooms! We've never had a problem like this before! I can't believe you'd treat my home like this!

This panicked us, and instead of dealing with it there and then, I said nothing. Just curled up into this ball of silent anxiety.

Much like I did when I was bullied at school. When anything went wrong in my life. I thought if I was silent and crept about trying to struggle on, everything would become bearable.

It didn't.

What is odd about sinking back into a dark illness that you've had before, is that you don't recognise the warning signs until it is too late.

This is something I wrote just before I got ill again, similar in tome to the diary entry I made at the end of 2004 (see Chapter 5). I haven't over-analysed it, but I guess once the brain starts drowning, the remnants of goodness try to fight the illness.

A LETTER OF POSITIVITY TO ONESELF

You are a brilliant person.
I can see it now.
You've hidden it from yourself, but you like yourself deep down.
You know how important it is to your health to feel good about being you.
You don't ever have to feel bad again.
I'm putting my foot down!

We've come a long way, but we can go further.
If you catch yourself fretting or getting anxious, know You come first.
You are better than It!
You don't have to dwell on the negativity of the past, or past thoughts or actions.

They're still there but they mean nothing.

And it's not even about morals or being a great guy (although you are) and handsome.

In fact, all those hidden bits of yourself that only others may see; your eyes are open to them now. So when you catch yourself feeling angsty or feeling bad about how you look or obsessing over details or thoughts, trying to fit made-up rules, or feeling desperately sad about life or the human condition, the meaning of it all, the past or something that happened and you're too anxious to deal with it…

Come back to this place and say: I am Good and I Don't Deserve *These* Feelings after a Quarter of a Century feeling like a Nothing!

You don't have to put up with any external shit that makes you feel bad. There's nothing wrong with politely and calmly saying that you're not comfortable with *whatever it is*. Yes, perhaps people will see your flaws, but everyone has them. Stick up that your personal Bill of Rights again and Memorise It!

Most of all, remember that you are good, and that if you are in a place where you feel bad, don't stay there, not even for a second.

The bad feeling does not need to stay; you have permission to get away from it. For example, when you were anxious earlier, don't then say, 'Well That's It, Might As Well Rut In It And Get Depressed!'

Instead say, 'It isn't right to feel like this. I should feel at best Happy and at worst suitably Emotive, but always with the aim of contentment and getting to a healthy contented space.'

No more private despair, no matter what. It's better to appear

weird than sit miserable, unstable and quiet.
Speak up; you have an amazing way of speaking. If you communicated what you were feeling, you'd help other people, too!

Also, you have learned that your scars aren't anything to be ashamed of, and that deep introspection in a negative way will lead to illness. As will deciding to stay ill rather than work through the process of recovery.

So after 25 years, that's that.
No more dwelling. No more thinking you have to feel bad because of silly things, what people say, or what you think people have said.
The next time a bad thing happens or something makes you upset, come back here, to this positive place and you'll find me.

Waiting for you.

13.
RELAPSE

'It can't be that life is so senseless and horrible. But if it really has been so horrible and senseless, why must I die, and die in agony? There is something wrong!'

Leo Tolstoy, The Death of Ivan Ilych

I was determined to make my life in Witney work. Patty was as good as her word and she fulfilled everything I had asked for. So sweet she was, yet she had her own life, a life she'd forged in Witney. She liked to go to work, socialise locally, and live a homely life. I didn't really want to do that. I wanted to be creative, to go into Oxford and meet like-minded people.

My attempts at getting into the Oxford lifestyle were futile. I went to a gay pub, where all my pints were bought for me and I even played the pub quiz. It was a pleasant enough evening, even when a drunken man from the nearby homeless shelter tried to come in and queer-bash. Luckily the police were called. I was proud of the barman who stood up to this really scary homeless man, yet any attempted follow up with the acquaintances I'd made at that pub amounted to nothing.

Making friends in Witney was hard. It was an automaton town, robots going about their daily life, refusing to interact with one another. Perhaps I had stumbled upon some kind of conspiracy... oh no, wait. That's the plot to *The World's End*.

I could not have guests over as the ever malevolent Landlord forbad it. He behaved like a freak, stalking the house, slamming doors and peering through cracks. It made for a very unwelcoming atmosphere. You felt you were imposing just by using the kitchen. This was a privilege I paid £400 a month for. This is only as true as subjectivity can ever be. I am certain that anyone who has met this man in his home would tell you he was odd and more than a little territorial, but he was no tyrant. He might have been weird and a little odd, but he was no monster. He made things socially awkward, but my anxiety was in any case at 90%, and I spent my time either with Patty in the attic or in my own freezing and uninsulated room. I never felt I could use the kitchen and most of my meals became reduced price Boots' sandwiches. I hadn't noticed but I had begun to lose weight. When I visited home later that month, my parents remarked on how gaunt I looked. I didn't really pay any notice at first, still thinking I had a gut, so it couldn't be that bad. I often joke now I am 'more than healthy' in my weight, that the best way to diet is through a complete mental breakdown. Nilsen wasn't very happy with Ben staying, and I didn't want Ben to be treated like he was something bad, so he only ever stayed when the landlord went on long trips to Nepal to patronise the villagers.

Within a few months of living there, I had become thoroughly miserable. But I was determined to stick it out. I didn't want to be like other people that I knew who had given up and gone back to their parents because they couldn't hack 'independence'.

I had lovely times with Patty, but they were brief reprieves from personal darkness. She couldn't be my entire social circle and I didn't want her to be. I tried everything in my power to stick it out. I volunteered, on my days off, at the Oxfam Bookshop, a few doors down from the one I was paid to work in. The people there were friendly and I was optimistic that I would make friends. The only guy there that was my age, however, seemed deeply autistic and never really spoke to me. I joined the local Morris Dancing side (warning signs) where there were lots of cool people to be made acquaintance with. Angela, a Northern engineer, was particularly kind and picked me up in her car every week. I started to do CBT (cognitive behavioral therapy), to try to live more in the moment. I kept a positivity jar. I wasn't happy though, I was miserable, a self-imposed misery I could have left, but yet I made myself stay the course, with all the myriad crutches just about getting me through the day.

What nobody knew about at the time were my endless crying fits. I'd just start a gentle weeping which would eventually turn into a full animalistic sobbing. I didn't realise that this was an obvious sign of a breakdown. The same thing had happened at the beginning of 2005 when I was hospitalised. But no, on I went, a bit like driving with flat tyres. Eventually you're going to fuck the suspension. I can still pinpoint the exact moment my brain went into death mode.

It was my 25th Birthday. Scruff took me for coffee in the delightfully nightmarish environs of Milton Keynes, its grid-like road system comforting me no end. I'd been waffling on as usual, my anger forming into endless meandering monologues that twirled, fell and backspun. I never knew quite what I was talking about at times like those. I was simply annoyed at the fact that I hadn't got a tiara and champagne to wake to or something equally bizarre. I was annoyed at the way people seemed to be walking too fast. I was annoyed at the fact that I had to make small talk with a heterosexual work friend with a Polish fiancée I had bumped into in H M Samuels.

I kept on about how unhappy I was with my life. I'd say things like 'I don't understand why it has to be like this,' and 'I can't believe you'd treat me in such a way,' with more and more cryptic permutations. This caused Scruff, who found himself having to look after me single-handedly over the Christmas period, to question my delusions. He was trying so hard to get through to me. He explained later how scared and upset he was to see me so ill. He was a brilliant support though, and did an amazing job in an impossible situation. I remember texting an acquaintance to ask why I was so unhappy, and they replied that I perhaps thought about my Self too much.

This Was The Moment, People! It hit me. After this I lost my appetite. They thought it was flu.

When I returned to my little room in Witney, my crying fits became daily outbursts, then hourly. I looked over my 2012 diary in which I had got other people to write my entries for me in an attempt to be less introspective, and wept at how sweet people had been, and how thoughtful. I wept at how selfish I was, how self-obsessed, and how disillusioned that a career in the media now meant nothing.

I was prescribed Citalopram: first at 10mg, then 20mg, and finally 40mg. I became convinced I was dying of something, growing more and more weak, wandering to the doctors in floods of tears. I collapsed on the floor in front of Patty, convinced I had pneumonia. Back and forth from London to Witney. Assessments, Assessments, Assessments. Barely able to swallow food, panic attacks, constant confessing of loneliness and isolation; that I noticed a pattern in my behaviour, of avoiding people, being combative, oppositional.

All through this Ben rang me every day, several times. I could barely talk, wouldn't make sense, but he was always so calm and his sweet tones gave me moments of reprieve from this agony. I rang him sometimes at 3a.m just to cry down the phone. He'd listen and speak slowly and calmly back. How did I deserve such loyalty?

It was the worst anxiety and obsessive turmoil I'd ever been in. What was even worse for my mum was that whilst I was banging my head against the radiator, she'd also received news that her sister Carol had just been found dead in her home, from the apparent effects of long-term alcoholism. It fell to her and Aunt Vicky to plan the funeral together. Added to that, my sister was being pursued by her ex-Pig with the threat of legal action, and dodgy people knocking threateningly on the door. It was a stressful time for the family. Never rains.

Convinced I was dying of a myriad of illnesses, I now wanted to die. I kept getting flashes of throwing myself off the top of one of the tall buildings near Clapham Junction. I was convinced my cognitive functions and memory had gone.

And yet life goes on, which I didn't realise in my state. Experiences horrific and beatific are equally real and valid. You are as alive and present in both. It doesn't mean you're dead if the experience is bad. Something mad in my head. The most depressing day was, naturally, Aunt Carol's funeral. My Uncle turned up toothless and with a strange girlfriend who looked like the freak from *The Morgana Show*. The crematorium was packed with people from the Tesco where she had worked and was a nice send off. In her eulogy, I'd accidentally included a memory that my late Aunt collected cat ornaments, something the vicar read out, but it transpired that it wasn't true at all.

The wake, with extended family members we didn't speak to and awkward silences, and me not being able to sit still, they weren't nice things. Seeing how ill and weird my family looked was deeply unpleasant. My mum so wanted me to get well. I tried for her sake to shake the constant thoughts that my brain was rotting in my skull. I tried to walk about on my own. So unsure of myself, my dad affixed snow-grips to my Doc Martens. It was such a bitter winter, early 2013. The snow covered everything. That was the worst of it.

At one low point I was ready to lay my head on the tram tracks, so I called 999 and was rushed to A&E, but discharged when my blood tests came back normal. I had demanded them as I was still convinced of some cancer.

'I can't wave a magic wand,' the duty doctor kindly informed me.

My editor and his editorial friend have suggested that this section of the book might not end up being as funny as the first half and might even seem a little bleak. Therefore, in my attempt to lighten it, I'll throw a few gags in here. Like this one:
What do you call a Russian man with three balls?
Hoodya Nicabolokov.
See? Gold!

I tried my best to kick start a recovery, which of course you can't. It has to happen naturally.

I tried to be creative.

I'd start files on my computer, but all I managed of any length was this, which I spent hours agonizing over:

The Furry Dumpling

John was a dumpling. That much we can deduce from his obvious physical structure. Yet the fact that he was a dumpling didn't hold him back from undertaking all of life's chores. He had his share of work to do on the plate which was his home with all the other dumplings. He had to do cooking, cleaning, vacuuming and such; it was a Marxist commune, all in all.

The thing is, John did more than his fair share. He liked to do as much as possible, smearing himself about in his slimy residue, up and down the delightfully patterned plate world. Added to which he was furry, much as the title suggests. Now an over-eagerness to impress and a hirsute constitution meant that he was envied by the depilated dumpling folk of Plate World. They were jealous of his spins and tumbles and excellent mopping;

But something turned in me.

I thought, 'You're not going to kill yourself, so go back to Witney and get back to your job.' And I did, for two weeks. Ben tells me now, he wished he'd taken the decision for me to say not to go back, that I was too ill and the job wasn't important, my health was much more so. He shouldn't have felt any guilt. Having seen my friends in similar situations as I was in, it's impossible to know what to say or do to help someone in this turmoil.

The first week I still cried and had childlike fits of

despair and anguish, feeling worthless and ugly, crying and screaming at myself in the mirror. The second week I felt like a child in a cleaner, purer way, making Lego models and doing the crossword, doing my few hours in the shop. I really loved it.

Then it came crashing down again. I became convinced that my digestive tract wasn't working, and feeling pitiful, I drank heavily with Patty, not knowing where it would take me. I got so drunk that I wandered alone in the dark streets for hours. I passed out, and woke up in an alleyway with my clothes ripped not knowing what had happened to me.

After a rather vulgar display in the doctor's surgery, came a rare outburst when I smashed the waiting room mirror, and then ran out, resulting in the police forcing me to attend a psychiatric assessment, where I confessed to the horror of the night before. They offered little sympathy, those two doctors. Blimey! Of all the assessments (and I have had several) Dr. Smith and Roy were like Lynchian cardboard cutouts hastily assembled to tick the boxes. All this still seemed unreal to me. Ben saved me from this horror, as I told him the state I was in and he came down in his car straight away.

There were still more crying fits. Within 48 hours, I'd handed in my notice at both my jobs, which in the current economic climate and my ability to be part of this workforce, shouldn't be taken lightly. I also gave up my room, having seen what reality was really like for me on this spinning blue orb, and my place in it… Ben took me to a flat he'd bought for us to live in together. But when I got there, my fits didn't stop and I still felt terrible. I just screamed, 'This is all life is. People living in houses and sleeping. That's all!' I said over and over.

I was trying desperately to find the wherewithal to do myself in. Slowly walking in front of moving cars, tying my neck to the door-handle, sending ominous suicidal goodbye texts. I even tried to spray solvent down my neck, to ensure death. I knew none of it was fail-safe. I was in such agony, I genuinely wanted to die. I would've done anything to cease.

I held my breath and pushed my face deep into the pillow every night hoping, by accident, that I'd suffocate or choke on my own tongue. Whenever I did start to suffocate, of course, the natural reflexes of self-preservation and freeing the airways got in the way. Or got out of the way, if you want to be pedantic.

The worst pain is, of course, love. To not love anyone or anything, to have that bit of you killed or deadened would make the process of extinguishing your life easier. What's worse is to still feel love for everyone, and to not want to live. To know how much it will hurt them, and how much you miss them, being stuck inside that bell jar. There isn't torture like that on the market.

So, it was suggested, I come home to Ma and Pa, where memories of my quarter century plagued my mind, memories of my chronic masturbating, laziness and night terrors lay.

I still wanted to die.

One night I'd convinced everyone I was well enough to be left alone.

That was the night I got the closest to ending my own life.

With a noose around my neck ready to attach it to a sturdy wall-fixture, I pushed down on the tight fabric around my throat and could feel it suffocating me. But still the human body wants to live on, even if the brain is mush.

Clever human body.
Because the brain didn't stay mush.
I got better.
I. Got. Better.
Three gorgeous words that bear repeating.

As a coda to this chapter, Ben wanted me to include in big bullet points what to do when you feel you're getting to the point of the breakdown I have just described. (Obviously the earlier the better).

THINGS TO DO WHEN YOU'RE HAVING A BREAKDOWN

- Get signed off work immediately.
- Take things very easy.
- Stay in a safe environment with supportive friends / family nearby.
- Talk to your G.P. (but don't take what they say as gospel; it's fine to question and take control over your treatment. You can always get a pushy friend to help, here).
- Be around people who understand the situation you're in, and make sure you don't do silly things, like drink too much or hurt yourself.
- Know that it will end, and that you will get better.

14.
RECOVERY

> 'True happiness is to enjoy the present, without anxious dependence upon the future, not to amuse ourselves with either hopes or fears but to rest satisfied with what we have, which is sufficient, for he that is so wants nothing. The greatest blessings of mankind are within us and within our reach. A wise man is content with his lot, whatever it may be, without wishing for what he has not.'
>
> *Seneca*

I once believed that the only logical consequence of the events of my life was suicide. Yet my brain somehow switched from this perception of my own limited mortality to its polar opposite, a real desire to live with purpose. The switch came in the space of one single morning, after three months of hell.

At the time, I was laying in bed, unable to sleep. I was still googling various illnesses, convinced I had some undiagnosed brain-tumour or terminal façade, when I thought I might as well, for balance, check if there was anything to be said about any of the recent mental health diagnoses I'd spied in my medical records.

One term that had popped up a few times was 'Emotionally Unstable Personality Traits', something I had never really given much thought to. I hadn't even made the connection that this was the European term given to the misleadingly phrased Borderline Personality Disorder. So I thought I'd type it into Google, and see what popped up.

Well, well, well!

I was amazed to find this documentary put together by an American University, where people had described having the disorder. They talked about mood swings, the need to be around people, or going to extreme lengths to be with people whenever they felt lonely. The emptiness, the extreme reactions to emotional states, the self-destructive behaviour. All those years of thinking I was some damaged man-child who could never grow up. That these extremes of mood were just me somehow being immature or just not bothering to control them. That I was a grade A fuck-up. Now it all, suddenly, made sense. There was something there now. Something concrete.

The worst part of the breakdown for me had been that it was all agonisingly unsolvable. I desperately wanted to climb out of the hole I was in, but there seemed to be no tangible conceptual stepping stones. The walls that led up out of the hole were completely smooth. There was nothing to grab onto. This acknowledgement of traits that had been touched upon and reiterated by mental health professionals over the years, finally made sense to me. It's one thing to be diagnosed with an illness. What's most important about it, isn't the fact that you now have a label, an excuse, a get out of jail free card, 'Look, I Can't Be Blamed - I'm Mental.' No it's not that, because I don't care about the label. It's the *diagnosis* that is the first step to recovery.

Now I have a diagnosis that fits, and makes sense to me, I can look further to see how others have dealt with it, and start to forge a new life for myself.

Once I truly accepted that I had traits of a borderline personality (as outlined in a psychiatric report) I began to do some research into it. A lot of the problems I've had in my life, which I couldn't explain before, and thought were me being some fuck-up, now made sense. My mood swings, my emotional sensitivity, the feelings of emptiness, intense friendships and obsessive behaviour, this was how and where I had been. Still, despite a history of hospitalisation and self-harm, having met a lot of other people with the condition, I consider myself to be quite a high-functioning person with a PD. Ultimately I am, as the author of *Girl, Interrupted* Susanna Kaysen said of BPD, 'just like everyone else, except our emotions and personality are amplified'.

I often think people have elements of mental illness in themselves. It's obvious, when you think about it. The human body comes into contact with bacteria all the time which could lead to a physical illness, whether it's diagnosed or not. It's the same with mental illnesses, only due to stigma, it is actively hidden, or so entwined with who we 'are', that it goes unnoticed or is subsumed in something else.

One particular problem that I'm still trying to overcome at the moment is how I interact with new people. I see myself as a giving person, and I perceive the needs of others as greater than they probably are. If I can give my time or attention to someone I will. It's my hero Quentin Crisp's first law, or one of them anyway. This can become problematic if you're in a situation that is potentially dangerous. I like people, I like to be social and talk to people and I will talk to most. If they appear nice, I will give them the world! I can't really say no, which is dangerous. So my main coping mechanism if things go weird is to cut the interaction Dead, there and then!

When it gets messy is with my constant changing of moods and outlooks, feeling great suddenly, feeling invincible. You could end up spending the evening talking to a heroin addict under some railway cuttings. I like to talk to people online, and sometimes they want to meet up. These people could be anyone, couldn't they? I've seen *Catfish*; it's terrifying, and 90% of the time it goes no further than mindless banter. But then there is the other ten per cent, due to the way online communication works. People can transform themselves from their own Alan Bennett domestic ordinariness to a Burroughsian nightmare.

I don't want any of this. I don't want to create some oblique acquaintances with strangers. I also feel I am betraying my real friends and family. I also feel I am 'leading on' the people I talk to online, as there isn't any real possibility of a stable friendship with me. I'll be obsessed with them for a week or two, will write them poems and buy them lunch, then within a fortnight they'll make me sick and I'll want to destroy any connection we ever had. They are fast-food friendships. Ones I don't need to keep the PD in check for. It's not fair on them, me or anyone else. I suppose I am writing this as a Warning to them so when I next get into the 'All the world is an online friend' headspace I can send them this passage from the book.

It also serves as an apology and explanation for the myriads of people whom I've stood up, lied to or disappeared from.

Having said all this, and I'm sure it may come as a surprise, I still can manage to be a good friend and have stable, loving and fulfilling friendships and relationships with people. This is with the friends that can accept my craziness, or ride the wave of it, the ones I try my best to keep focused on, and the ones that are consistent and wonderfully unique.

* * *

It was time to take my health seriously. All this was fizzing in my mind just from watching the documentary. I was so relieved that there was this dim speck of hope for me. I didn't sleep that night. I have heard it is good to reset the body with 24 hours of sleep deprivation.

I went out with my laptop to the local coffee shop, and read more on my condition. Then I felt another flicker of hope. As if the neurons and synapses were starting to come back together in my shattered mind. Perhaps this was also the citalopram too. It was all beginning to gel. And only a day ago I was tying a belt around my neck and trying to attach it to the door handle.

The other flicker of hope was creativity. Going to Witney had almost killed that. I had given up big time on my outlet. My brain kept telling me that the only purpose to make art was to create some great political change, à la Orwell. Anything other than that wouldn't fit the bill. These were realistic standards to set oneself. I hadn't considered that being creative was my bag, was what made me. Other people liked horse-riding, were pole-vaulters, interior decorators, go-go dancers or goblin impersonators. My bag was to make plays, radio-shows and films. To make ideas come to life, to entertain and amuse. To play characters that said silly things. To direct other people's work and maybe bring people together.

This thing I'd killed in myself was the very spark that could keep me going. I had got confused along the way. Confused that just because my stuff wasn't 'commercial' or 'polished' it was somehow 'wrong', 'bad' and irrelevant. I hadn't thought I could tell people to fuck off, and just do it because I wanted to do it.

I looked through my online portfolio and saw all the amazing things I'd achieved. The plays I'd directed, one-on-one performances, taking a show to Edinburgh, the web series and all the other bits 'n' pieces. I felt a glow inside me, for the first time in years.

I made a promise to myself at that moment that if I wrote a few pages of a play a day I could say to myself that I had achieved something.

I kept my word and in a month I'd produced a screenplay and a full-length retelling of *The Owl & The Pussycat*. It was remarkable, that transformation. Still, I took things very easily.

I started eating properly. Actually, I ate like a man starved. I slept better and the chattering negative voices in my head Stopped. This did seem like a first. Because ever since I can remember being capable of creative thought, there had been that negative voice, that controlling voice, that narrow, rigid voice that had somehow made me do things in such a convoluted miserable way. That had made me react all the time and make a real hash of things.

That voice had gone.

I felt real.

I felt the love of my family and friends, and I could now feel that my love for them was genuine. Depression had robbed me of all of that. I said to my mum, when I started to feel better, that being ill was like viewing everything from the end of a long tunnel. Every conversation had been like the person opposite me could've been miles away. I could hardly hear what people said, nor take any warmth from hugs or kindnesses.

Being part of the real world once more, made me able to enjoy things. I felt relieved and grateful. I was happy just because I wasn't ill. Eating a meal, drinking a cup of coffee, having a conversation, taking a shower. It was all so gorgeous. Electric.

I'm not acting like everything was perfect the moment I realised. I had lots of issues to work through, issues that I'm still dealing with, but now I would be capable of working through them, whereas before I had been totally lost.

So much had changed. I was now open about how I felt and could describe it in a way that was less harmful to me. I now understood my extreme reactions to things was part of the disorder, and I wasn't now as upset by it. By telling people I felt rough, they could be understanding, or not, but at least it would now be out there in the open, and it wouldn't just be me struggling in silence.

I felt such compassion for people and for myself. I felt the world's equal. I accepted my limitations that having the disorder brought, and paradoxically, felt myself now really able to live my life the way I wanted. No longer would I force my own narrative of happiness.

My impulsivity remained, as did my mood swings. I almost gave into them more in a way, knowing they would pass, rather than rigidly hold myself together all the time I was having them. I'd have down days, but now I wouldn't dwell on them. I'd take care of myself. I'd play a game or read a book, and if I couldn't do that I'd lay down and watch the television, or listen to music, or just lay there knowing it was much better to do that than go down a self-destructive miserable route.

Another thing I did and continue to do (though like brushing your teeth, you can always do it more often And Floss As Well!) was to attend a peer support group, in this case the SUN project, which met locally for people with Personality Disorders. It was a lifeline to be with people who had the same problems, and was a great support. It was also good to support others.

I took up the one-man show idea again, performing it first at The White Bear Theatre, to which I invited Debbie, a lovely person who was putting on an LGBTQIA+ festival, and loved the play so much that she asked me to perform it again for them as part of the *Freedom To Be* Festival. That really made me happy, to be in demand. To have my family come and see me being hale and hearty. A transformation.

I took more care to help my parents and be less rude to them, but not in a rigid, 'I must be polite always'. If there were any problems or arguments I would take them more at face value.

I was asked by Kelly Jones to come and be part of a workshop with The National Theatre of Wales. When she emailed casually to tell me, I was so disbelieving I kept texting back to make sure it was still on. That was a fun week in Llandudno, hauled up in this big house with a load of actors, playing with C.B. radios (it's what we do in the arts, honey).

I had to play an abusive father in it. I had to butch up. It was très exciting.

Back in London I did more performances of the one-man show at The Lord Stanley in Camden. Such an odd venue with its ornate statuettes. It was during that time that I prepared another Shakespeare; a Queer version of Macbeth, that I had a lot of fun doing, and this time made sure I wasn't stressed during the making of it. One could argue that the outcome was a little sloppier than usual, but I don't know. I told myself I wouldn't get into any arguments or shit-storms during the making of it, and if it got too stressful I'd stop. That was new; I wouldn't force myself into illness.

When I was at Uni, being busy and running myself into the ground was synonymous with success. If people weren't commenting on how tired, busy and rundown I was, I wasn't doing my job properly. I was still very busy now, but took more time for myself, to have fun and do other extra curricular things; naughty things.

The anxiety lessened, too. My big avoidance thing abated. I wasn't going to put up with people's shit as much.

It still happened. There were still incidents and problems that made me feel anxious, but I was more able to put them to one side and not let them rule me or ruminate in my mind. This is something I've improved on a lot. I no longer take myself at the estimation other people have of me. I have forged my own identity beyond that. Although identity is the biggest problem of anyone with BPD, and the Borderliner's identity is an inconsistent and slippery thing.

My lifelong desire for a consistent personality, to be my own man and not constantly likened to Stephen Fry, dropped down my list of priorities. Now these are being healthy, enjoying life and helping other people, if I can. I no longer fret that I am living at home, or that certain things are not being fulfilled just because society tells me they're not. I've enjoyed the things I've been doing, rather than just doing them because I have to do them or because the voice tells me to do them.

I kept doing the one-man show, doing the Camden Fringe and the Hot August Fringe. Then in 2014 we 'toured' it, starting in Oxford where Patty, my old creepy Landlord and the other stalwarts of the bookshop came to see it. It was brilliant for me, as I still feel the play is a signifier of my health and purpose. 'Look he can stand for an hour and play 22 characters!' If that isn't a sign of a balanced mind, what is?

I still have bad days and weeks, though nothing near as bad as the breakdown. Nothing prolonged. I'd tell someone as soon as I noticed it getting that way. I hope I would, in any case, because the illness is so clever that it changes your perception of reality. Maybe I wouldn't notice the getting worse. I have the odd really bad day. They come once in a blue moon when I think I'm sliding back. I'm no saint and I've been guilty of some negative behaviour, but I work on that. I tell people I'm in a constant state of recovery. Like the alcoholic, who is always an alcoholic.

Guilt is something I'm guilty of. I hurt people and I need to confess sometimes. I think it's better not to tell everyone every sordid detail, though. Some things in life aren't that important. I haven't detailed every bowel movement between these pages, tempted as I have been to do so.

One of the qualities I admire in people is the ability to live in the present moment. To say yes to things if they can, and go with any new experiences and adventures that the decision brings. This is something I still like to do. I also like to try and get round to doing things I've wanted to do for a long time. For instance, since my breakdown at the beginning of 2013, I've hopped from project to project, and there hasn't been a week when I haven't been working on something new. What's more fun is that people you meet during one project then become involved or can even create the idea for the next one.

I've met wonderful new people such as Alice, my French *amie*, when I worked on her short film *Once Upon A Star*, or the extremely cute playwright D D Armstrong, when I directed his play *You Know What You Are* for Black History Month, or the less cute Leon Fleming when I directed his short piece *Boris Got Buggered* in which I cast Menno, an ageing Dutch stringbean. He ended up working with Pallas who I met at the SUN group in an even shorter play *Must Sunday Come At All* performed at The Drayton Arms, and which involved a cucumber, an alien crab, a doctor's surgery and a giant wormhole.

What comes across is not just the projects but the people. I love the people and being with them. I am a socially awkward animal; one that loves people one moment and hates them the next, completely irrationally, due to my brain. Hate is a strong word. I rarely hate. It's fairer to say that I become exhausted through interaction or boredom, and then overexcited and obsessed to be in the presence of others. I always thought it was because I was bad at being sociable, but I can occasionally set the table aroar.

Being overly busy is unnecessary now, and I sometimes like to have time off. I still need something to go to though, to keep my mind occupied. I need to keep an eye out to check that my mental health M.O.T. is in date. We should all do this really, as otherwise bad habits will rear their heads.

Another thing I've learnt about the process is that whole 'it'll pass' mantra that people wheel out. *The bad mood will pass.* I think this is too simple. For me it's, 'You're fucking pissed off and fucked up in the head now and everything is wrong, but that's okay. It's okay to feel like that and you're just as valid and alive when things are shit as when they're good.'

For some reason I had told myself in the past that anything ugly or unpleasant in the feelings department was *ipso facto* not part of life, as you weren't actually living or experiencing it. When certain relationships with people you're very close to and perhaps in love with, or related to by blood - when these people annoy you or behave in a way that is unfair or does not compute, this can put the brain in such a whirr, that one can behave like a twat and make an awkward situation a million times worse. I refer the right honourable gentlemen to the previous comment. That was a new one, and I still have to remind myself of it regularly.

But now the cycle has been broken.

My life from the age of ten was a narrative that was pleasing and that I was obsessively trying to pull into shape. I was obsessed with exercising control over it.

Now I'm no longer looking to create that narrative with my own life. I don't look that far ahead. I'm not obsessed with what might lie along the path less travelled. All my childhood fears of death, destruction and the end of our species that used to terrify me and keep me awake at night, they no longer worry me. The fear of death has gone. That is a bold statement to write, but it's true. I'm trying to conjur up the eternity of nothingness, and doing it made me go 'hmm' but not to panic. It's not ideal to be dead, but I won't be there to be part of it, so it's not really worth thinking about. That is my philosophy in a nutshell, really. Absurdism. No point even entertaining the notion of a 'god', as it has nothing to do with living life on this planet.

I do think a preoccupation with death is a by-product of depression. The vulnerability and fear which dogged my early life is that. I could never countenance the fact that this was all I thought and felt, and that it ran through everything I wrote and achieved like a stick of rock. These words that I'm typing out here on this document. That all this will come to dust. It doesn't bother me now. Life is a process. It's the moment in which we live our lives. You can't keep things static. Once you accept it, life is good. I'm not trying to go all hippy-dippy. It's a fact of the causality of time really, the Hayflick effect, entropy.

I just go with it now.

As far as my own life goes, I don't know what will happen in my future, or the future in general. It may well all be doom and gloom, but I am not going to engage with the unrealised. I shall go on creating projects, meeting new people and having new experiences. I will live my life in the present moment, and say yes to people if they want me to direct something for them, perform with them or write something for them.

Just like this book.

15.
A HOPEFUL ENDING

'Art is Life.'

George Eliot

I'm sure you're expecting more narrative here, but you're not going to get it. I'm sorry. Too much of an expected thing leads to listlessness and, I'm told, morbid obesity. So as we meander towards the final pages, let me provide you with a chapter that is rarely expected in this quadrant of the 21st century. An optimistic and, dare I say it, hopeful ending.

'It seems like a lot of these negative behaviours are a form of self-harm. Now you don't cut, you're finding other ways to hurt yourself,' Alex said. My diminutive Italian therapist with slick-backed hair and a knitted waistcoat has been a life-preserver these last few months. My life has been so much better since my breakdown. The obsessive voice in my head has stopped. I've been less anxious around confrontation. I've allowed myself to enjoy relationships, and developed healthy coping mechanisms for the rather unpleasant symptoms of BPD, but I still have low periods. I still have problems.

The problem that seems to have been a lifelong irritant is that for some reason I Do Not Like Myself. I used to be a lot worse, of course. I used to pride myself on my particular brand of self-hatred. I don't do that anymore. I try not to talk negatively about me. I try not to blame myself too much. I got over the fact that I don't think myself that attractive by simply not looking at myself anymore. I didn't do much on actively liking myself however. I can do the theory, I just can't do the practice.

*   *   *

Then something clicked.

Suddenly.

Flicking through my photos on Facebook, as one does, recalling incidents of giant seagulls stealing my ice cream on Brighton Pier, or dressing up as a zombie in an abandoned hotel in Holborn, I smiled. I looked at myself, my photoed image in various guises, lights, shapes and weights over the last few years, and thought, 'You look rather good, Simon. Yes, a good-looking boy,' and I meant it. I felt it. It wasn't forced, or theoried, or reasoned, or cajoled through CBT. I just felt it. I felt attractive.

A few weeks later trying on waistcoats for some Doctor Who Cosplay (don't ask) I saw myself in the mirror and went, 'Ooh, what a dish!' - and meant it! It wasn't latent narcissism and I didn't suffer some uncontrollable erection - I just felt good about the way I looked. I was stunned! How did this happen?

For the last quarter of a century, whenever I saw myself in photos or in a reflective surface, I felt a cringe, a surge of embarrassment, disgust, nausea or unhappiness. I never felt anything positive.

Something new had happened. It was a profound

moment, and it dislodged something in my mind, because a week after, I expressed in therapy thoughts about being bullied in the past.

I had been bullied at University, but I didn't want to touch too heavily on it here because I'd let it go by then, and didn't want to drag it up to try and make sense of it. However, I realised I hadn't come to terms with it till now, as I now see that those who sought to talk about me negatively and find ways of making me miserable in my day to day life at Uni, really had some deep problem in their own lives. I knew the theory, as when they'd been friends they'd confided about their anxiety problems, being bullied themselves, or paranoia, but now I realise they were taking it out on me to fulfil some need in their own sorry existence.

It offers me such freedom to see this as true rather than to try and convince myself in a theorised way (perhaps years of the 'convincing' caused me to become convinced).

I am free of my father, too. At the beginning of this year he had given up the alcohol and chronic cannabis use that made him intolerable in the evenings. The two habits have crept back in, and the other day I noticed a bong-like instrument under the computer desk. Ho hum. But why fret if he's returning to his intoxicated ways, where he will blather unpleasant nonsense into my ear till a liver disease claims him. The freedom comes from me.

I have decided I can no longer help him. He doesn't want help. He doesn't want a son either, really. He may require someone to agree with his narrow world view, to listen to his interests, forgive his many flaws, his verbal outbursts, someone to cook for him and to buy him beers when he's late in from work, but he is and perhaps always will be unprepared to act like a selfless adult to his son, which is a shame, as I would be happy to play the son role if he could just be bothered to pay lip-service to his adult father role.

I will remain open to him if he decides to change, but I am moving on with my life. I don't listen to his ramblings or get upset by them any longer. I block them out or do something else. I felt guilty when the e-book version of this paperback was released, as I felt I had written 'nasty' things about him. I went so far as to recant in an apologetic blog:

I had to touch upon my family. It's difficult because my parents are shy and private people. They don't want to be written about in a book. Unfortunately they have a right show-off as a son. I was forever showing them up as a child, saying inappropriate things at parties, repeating their private conversations to the wrong people at the wrong time. I'm sorry for that.

I was well aware of all this going into the book, so I tried to write as fairly as I could about my family. I included the silly details not to embarrass them, but to humanise them. I was writing passages at times when I was infuriated with my kith and kin, but what struck me the most when recounting these events, was that a pattern began to emerge. It showed that my parents were always there for me. They had helped me through breakdowns, taken me to Uni, paid for my flat, encouraged me, helped me and picked up the pieces, time and time again. Sure they were annoying, and there were problems here and there, ups and downs and all that, but ultimately they are good and decent people. It's true.

My mum is yet to read the book. My dad has read (skimmed) the first 19% (ebook stat) and commented, 'Oh it says I'm suffering from Post Traumatic Stress Disorder, and that I never paid any attention to you.' I tried to defend it by saying, 'Look at all the nice stuff I've written about you.'

I have tears in my eyes at the idea that my parents or anyone else would think I was trying to write nasty stuff about them and put it out in the world, though I accept that maybe I have.

This book feels like the turning point for a lot of things in my life. It's odd because in a lot of ways I've never felt closer to my parents.

Can I recant my recantation? What's that - a double recant? Because although the above is true, I want to be stronger than my father. He is a damaged man who was treated like dirt by an abusive man, my paternal grandfather, a criminal who was in prison when he was born.

My father had a terrible upbringing, followed by a lengthy naval career. He's had a miserable early-life, and I feel some empathy for him for that. We could have talked any number of times about it. I have offered to help, have let go, and have turned a blind eye to a myriad of things he has done over the years. And yet, at 54, although mellowed, he remains selfish and wilfully blind to the effect his absenteeism has had.

I did say I was over it, didn't I?

I am the next generation. I am different from my family. First to go to University, First to take a career in the arts. First to be openly affectionate, extrovert and loud. The first not to succumb to alcoholism or alcohol dependency. The first to be proud about themselves and their sexuality. The first to go into therapy. The first to acknowledge mental health problems. The first to work on their own issues of self-esteem. The first to accept that there is a world beyond one's own limitations or expectations.

I have revised my view of the world.

I no longer want to spend my time with people who bore me. I am not going to be compromised by needy dispositions.

I do like to speak to new people and help where I can. I think that will be a new career path for me. I was sitting in group therapy just a few hours ago, and the subject of work came up. Other members of this support group are lawyers, computer programmers and the like. I describe myself as 'self-employed' or 'in the arts'. Today I was thinking, 'I'd like to do something completely different'. I had another of these lightning bolts of optimism, of a future (I've never believed I or any of us had a future, I thought we'd just slide into a collective abyss of nothingness and that'd be it) where I had a job, a job with meaning, and a job with purpose. I Want To Be A Therapist, I thought.

I can talk for England, but I could listen for Her, too. I've been at the front line and I've had both negative and positive experiences of therepautic care. I can be detached and intellectualise in a clinical sense, but I can also be caring, compassionate and intuitive about people's needs. I have the ability to be creative in working towards a solution with people.

I have always felt there wasn't any point planning for a future in terms of mortgages, cars, life-partners and savings accounts. I've lived hand-to-mouth since I was fifteen, scraping by on benefits, hand-outs, temporary-jobs and the kindnesses of strangers. But without realising it at the time, I fell so madly in love. I have been with the same man now for eight glorious years. And he doesn't seem to be going anywhere soon, even though he knows far more than the contents of this book!

We've talked about settling down in the country, and I've been reticent, but actually it's an exciting thought. To actually be stable, to be in a position where stability is an option.

I have to take that chance.

When I became, medically, an adult (y'know when the brain and balls stop growing) I'd catch myself thinking, 'You're so different to how you were as a child. your thoughts are different, as are your face and body. You're a different person.' It's eerie. What's even more shocking, is that the nihilistic, self-harming, internally homophobic and self-hating suicidal teenager that was me would never have thought that he'd turn into the happily camp, partnered graduate with a wardrobe of velvet jackets and two-toned brogues, not to mention a penchant for the theatre that is me now. He could never have known that he'd experience such happiness as falling in love and making love to another man, one that he's cried tears of longing and joy for. He'd never have guessed that he'd meet hundreds of arty, creative people just like him, who would make him laugh and laugh. That he would see foreign countries and work with brilliant comedians and actors. That he would write plays and shake hands with Michael Palin.

If that fourteen year old had become so ill that he'd acted successfully on his suicidal plans, he'd never have done and said and been all he could do and say and be. The leap from skinny, chronically anxious, chainsmoking loner to healthy, contented theatre-director seems bizarre, but it wasn't really a leap. It was a long arduous crawl, and you can only see how wonderful it all is when you get there, and only when you get there can you really look back and take in how far you've come. As much as a naval-gazing book can allow. It illustrates the fact that everything changes. It doesn't stay the same.

I was going to go as far as to say, 'Don't top yourself because things will get better,' but I don't believe that. If I had possessed a crystal ball at fourteen and seen my 28 year old self, I would also have seen the terrifying future breakdowns and humiliations. The traumas so horrendous I can't begin to write them down - it would be enough to send me over the edge. But when you go through it, you either survive or you don't. Some of that survival is down to grit and determination, the rest is just luck. There is no God to help or guide us unless we invent one, and then only a god you should take credit for, for inventing, to give the illusion of guiding and helping you.

I'm an absurdist, anyway. The idea of debating the existence of a deity is so irrelevant to me that I don't even want to discuss it. And while I've got a book to say it in, that goes the same for conspiracy theorists. You all talk utter shit. Can you just shut up and do something interesting with your lives. You're wasting your time. Go and volunteer for a charity or something.

Now that's all off my chest, it's time to wrap up with book with something brilliant.

I was getting to a really good place there with the whole, 'If I had a crystal ball at fourteen thing...' wasn't I? It was really singing, and it really felt like it was building to a crescendo, then I had to go and spoil it all with some cheap aphorisms about god, and then turning it into a pithy, queeny little rant. Ooh, ooh, no I have something good, wait for it, wait for it... here it is... here it is...

It's this –

I started my life being told that I was weak and weird, first by my classmates, then, when I could understand it, by society. My family weren't hell-bent on making me miserable, but their own low self-esteem rubbed off on me and added to the mixture. I took this all this in and before long I had pretty poor mental health. Life was also happening, and bullying, hospital stays and crap sex, but then I decided to change my thoughts and what I focused on. I decided that I was not 'weak' or 'weird' or if I was then these judgemental ideas were subjective. I realised that there were other qualities about me and about the world. That you can go out and explore it and its infinite possibilities. And just by filling out a form to go to college, or get a flat, or university, or a play, without really knowing what I was doing, just blindly going in with naivity and confidence I came out the other side, sometimes good, sometimes not so good.

I have already spent most of my life Knowing that I was nothing, and then Realising that that way of viewing myself was making me ill beyond function. I have experimented and found evidence to show that I am not nothing, or bad, or ugly, or worthless, so this knowing has become an idea or philosophy or hunch, despite its going down a peg or two, or three, now and again. I have been ambivalent. Sometimes feeling worthless and sometimes feeling purposeful, and the scales have see-sawed for years.

In the last few years the worthless weights have been crumbling, and the strong purposeful weights have gained added momentum. I Know now that I matter, that I am brilliant, and, if I can do it, so can you.

Right, that's your lot. I'm off to look at some porn - ethical porn mind you; yes it does exist. Google it.

AFTERWORD

'As a child, I dragged a dead squirrel home on a skateboard, cut it open and tried to look at its brain.'

Jessica Biel

They say a book is never truly finished; more so when the subject of the book is a living, breathing entity.

Since the electronic publication of 'Bastardography' in March 2015, I've been taken on a new journey. It's an unnerving feeling to know that strangers have read my words and judged them. Some people have been complimentary. Some could relate to the experience of homophobic bullying or mental ill health, and others were caught up by the teething issues first editions have. The first editions of old, when the printing-press was confined to set-blocks and inks, the kind my Grandfather used to work on in the fifties. They were filled with so many mistakes in terms of spelling, grammar and fact, that they would subsequently print little errata pamphlets to slip inside the covers of the latest D. H. Lawrence or G.K Chesterton.

A digital first edition, is more of a minus one edition, and you can have as many of them as you like. Updates and corrections can still be made to 'Bastardography' for as long as there are computers. This, of course, is a bit dangerous, because one could become obsessed, wanting to change that chapter where I waxed lyrical about some best friend I now hate, or reinstate the hilarious passage about a celebrity who is now dead and can't sue for libel. One sometimes has to say, enough is enough. A print edition secures this. You can't start fucking around with the text once it's gone to print.

There is something symbolic about this for me. I can let it go now. So many commented on the mistakes in the original digital 'Bastardography', which never bothered me (although I am sure they may have befuddled the reader). It was perhaps that some of the content was a bit bizarre, dirty or disturbing. That people preferred to concentrate on the superficial snags rather than what I was actually saying. A bit like when a tramp exposes his cock to you in a service-station forecourt at 2am, and you complain that the stitching on his herringbone is shoddy.

What's great now the book has been rewritten for print is that you can nip/tuck and add the odd observation you missed the first time round. You can also capitalise on the feedback readers give you.

What has been my favourite thing about writing the book is going to various LGBT+ societies up and down the country, and reading from my experiences. To tell young LGBT+ people that this lonely boy of fourteen went through all that hell. To show solidarity with young people today is a great thing. I've used the book to speak at many different kinds of events and places. It's really been a great tool to connect with different people.

Would I have written the book if I'd known how hard it was going to be? That it would take from the middle of 2013 to the arse-end of 2015, and months of solid work and self-doubt? Probably. Because they say everyone has one book in them, don't they? Who are these 'they' though? That's the worry. Perhaps we should seek them out and have a good old go at them. 'Oi, *They*, is that is your real name? What the flip is your problem, saying all this stuff as if you're the arbiter of anything? Well you're not, you're a flipping joke'!' To which they will, collectively, break down in tears.

Well, serves them right, the turds.

* * *

Right. That's been my life so far. Some good, some bad and some more to come. I don't know if I'll write about it though. For someone who feels they have to confess every detail of their life and share it, expose it and analyse it, it might be a novel idea to just keep shtum for the next 70 years.

Why don't you go and write your own Bastardography now, and if you publish it, send it to me and I'll read it. In fact it's only fair that you should be given the chance.

Now you've read mine, I can read yours.

Simon Caleb Jay

October 2015
Belfast International Airport

London: the future

Feminist terrorists have cut the world's population by 95% with a sustained onslaught of neutron bombing. The earth has been set slightly out of orbit, leaving, according to calculations by those still alive, just 2350 years before it burns up. The surviving élite of women scientists, as a testimony to the event, decide the world's years will be chronicled in reverse order from that year on.

It is 1909, 441 years after the bombing. Women are the ruling class, the Populite. Men the underclass, live and work together. Relations between men and women are forbidden, punishable by death. London is in the grip of the Republican Activists, a male anarchist group trying to wrestle local power from the Populite. Their hunger for equality has led to increased acts of terror and random violence.

Morda, a political dissident, is a man trying desperately to fight off his heterosexual urges. Rocassa Milo, his employer and the subject of his fantasies, is a woman blighted by the discovery that she is not like other women, and cannot bear children. She has consequently not been subjected to the unsexing of the national sterilisation process, and has become aware of unnatural urges that she must somehow control and remove, before she is discovered, reported and ultimately executed.

OUT NOW IN HARD COPY AND EBOOK FROM ZITEBOOKS

www.zitebooks.com

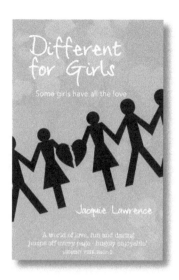

Different for friends

Fran and Cam, ecstatically reunited after a short break, but Cam faces the consequences of a random act she committed during their split.

Different for lovers

Gemma and Jude, new lovers torn apart by Gemma's fake fiancé. Just what is it about him that Jude has made it her life's mission to reveal?

Different for wives

Brooke and Nicola, married for seven years, are threatened by something and someone. But what and who is it?

Different for Girls

Enter a world where love, sex, and suspense meet betrayal, cruelty and heartbreak.
A world where the survival of love is all that matters.
A world where being different is the new normal.

OUT NOW IN HARD COPY AND EBOOK FROM ZITEBOOKS

www.zitebooks.com